"STOP FARTING IN THE PYRAMIDS"

And Other Things I Never Thought I'd Say or Do on the Path Toward Adulthood

"STOP FARTING IN THE PYRAMIDS"

And Other Things I Never Thought I'd Say or Do on the Path Toward Adulthood

By Katiedid Langrock

Creators Publishing
Hermosa Beach, CA

"STOP FARTING IN THE PYRAMIDS"
And Other Things I Never Thought I'd Say or Do on the Path
Toward Adulthood

Copyright © 2016 Creators Publishing

FIRST EDITION

Creators Publishing

737 3rd St

Hermosa Beach, California 90254

1-310-337-7003

ISBN 978-1-942448-93-8

CREATORS PUBLISHING

Contents

~ ~ ~

Preface

Writer by day (Catwoman by night), I have made a living working in the Hollywood entertainment industry for a decade. Four years ago, I was asked to write a weekly humor column. Since then, "Katiedid vs. ..." has been syndicated in newspapers across the country and internationally. This book is a compilation of these columns, following the changes in my life over the past four years. It chronicles two pregnancies, new motherhood, travel, my obsession with bluejeans and that painfully abstract notion and constant of growing up.

A little anecdote for you: When I was first coming up with the title for this book, I considered calling it "The Best of Intentions" because in my columns, as in my life, I have a tendency to mean well but ultimately fail with the greatest shade of flushed crimson cheeks. I landed on "Stop Farting in the Pyramids" not only because it stands as an excellent PSA (seriously, people, stop farting in pyramids) but also because the column that held this quote got me dropped from my first newspaper. At the time, it caused a tailspin, making me question everything about my columns, how I present myself and who I wanted to be publicly. Ultimately, I realized that the "Katiedid vs. ..." column could never and should never be greater or less than the sum of me, crimson cheeks and all. How freeing as a writer. And so, with the best of intentions, I offer it again here in these pages.

Thanks for reading, Mom! And thank you to all my other readers. I hope you enjoy.

P.S. Totally kidding about the Catwoman thing. Cats are terrifying.

http://WriteInTheWild.com

~ ~ ~

Chapter 1

The Birds and The Bees and The Cocks and The Bunnies: Sex

Rooster With Performance Anxiety

One month ago, a rooster showed up in my backyard. Maybe this isn't a strange occurrence for some of you, but I live in the city of Los Angeles. A homeless person showing up in my backyard? Sure. A starlet passed out after a coke binge in my backyard? Why not? But a rooster? Well, that's just crazy talk.

The runaway rooster and I did not get off to a good start. Our story was anything but love at first cluck.

It all started when I was jolted from my much-needed slumber by some type of crowing outside my window, just as the first glimmer of sunlight broke over the Hollywood Hills. But the crowing was a little odd; there was something not quite right about it. I couldn't place my finger on what type of bird was accosting my ears at this early hour.

Later that day, I saw the culprit -- a small, skinny rooster, taking a stroll through my backyard. I walked up to the little guy. "Hey, jerk, where'd you come from?" I yelled. "Why don't you take your poor excuse for an alarm clock elsewhere?"

In response, the rooster ruffled his feathers. He puffed up his chest. He opened his beak and let out a COCK-A-DOOoo. Very anticlimactic.

It was the same odd noise I had heard the night before. Not a full, robust COCK-A-DOODLE-DOO but rather a falsely confident COCK-A-DOOoo. It was as if someone had let the air out of my rooster's balloon. Could it be stage fright? Performance anxiety?

Unfettered, the cock tried again. He ruffled his feathers, puffed up his chest and started his strong crow, but just as he did last time, he lost his confidence, and the crow trailed off: COCK-A-DOOoo.

I immediately fell in love with him and named him Herman.

Herman remained fairly timid around me, but he decided to make my overgrown backyard home. He'd spend the days pacing and practicing his crow. Perhaps some would not find a little rooster fixated on perfecting his doodle-doos to be the world's best pet, but even when he was waking me up at 4 a.m. with his futile attempts to crow like Pan, I was still bemused by him.

Then, after about a week or so, Herman was gone.

A few days later, I was watching television, about to turn in for the night, when there was a tapping at my back window. Herman?!

I jumped off the couch and ran over to the door to find a fat ol' hen. Where are all of these chickens coming from?!

The hen, unlike my beloved rooster, was not shy. That girl flew right up to me and clucked away, rapidly and frantically: Buck. Buck. B'gah! I decided this must be Herman's girlfriend looking for her man. Naturally.

I named her Henrietta.

Henrietta was not a longtime visitor, but she was a frequent visitor. By day, she scoured my neighbors' lawns, searching for her dearly departed. By night, she'd return to my back window and tap on it until I came outside to hang out for a while.

Then, after a couple of weeks of nightly visits, she too disappeared.

I worried for my star-crossed lovers. Did they ever find each other? Were they doomed to the fate of Romeo and Juliet? Perhaps they sneaked onto a cruise ship and were now living large in Costa Rica, where the roosters aren't judged so fiercely for their crowing bravado and no one will think twice about a big fat chicken leading her scrawny man down the beach.

I hoped so. I worried so.

Until last night, when all my questions were answered. There was a tapping on my back window. I ran over to see both Henrietta and my beloved Herman. Henrietta clucked at Herman. Herman ruffled up his feathers. She clucked at him again. Herman puffed out his chest. Henrietta gave one last encouraging cluck. And my little Herman belted one out -- a loud, complete, boastful COCK-A-DOODLE-DOO.

As it turns out, all the little cock with performance anxiety needed was one good clucking.

The Coffee Shop Hooker

Coffee shops around the world have become overrun by hideous creatures known as writers. You know the type. They are found

4

hunched over, sipping on their third cup of coffee, black. They wear sweatshirts with mustard stains, which we can only assume came from the cookouts they were forced to attend, yellow reminders of the most recent time they spent any quality time outdoors. They wear caps over unbrushed hair, advertising some odd vocation or vacation, such as writer or Maine. They hide like bedbugs in the comfiest chairs in the joint, lurking behind laptops, never making eye contact.

I, too, make fun of these literary oddballs. But this week, I was struggling with my column. I just needed to get out of the house, get a new angle. I pulled on my mustard-stained hoodie and walked to my local coffee shop.

I was typing away at a column that was going nowhere, when in walked a lanky redheaded woman in her early 20s. She looked like your average coed until she was greeted by a short man in his late 40s, who had been lurking in the back corner, head buried in a newspaper. They shared an awkward hug/kiss/handshake and then sat down at the table next to mine.

My interest was piqued. Anything to aid my procrastination. Was this a meeting with an estranged father? How scandalous.

The man pulled out a resume and said, "I hope you don't mind meeting me here. I know it's unconventional."

Just a job interview. Yawn. I was about to transfer my attention back to my column, when I heard him say, "So, how long have you been hookering?"

I nearly spit out my latte.

I kept my eyes glued to my computer screen, but my ears were firmly and acutely attached to the conversation at the next table. It went like this:

John: Hooking, is that what you call it? I mean, how long?

Prostitute: About eight months.

John: Good, good. Do you like it?

My thoughts: Yeah. It's what she dreamed of doing as a little girl.

Prostitute: Excuse me?

John: I mean, do you find the work rewarding?

My thoughts: Sure she does.

Prostitute: Sure I do.

John: Phew. That's a load off. Your resume says you're attending college.

Prostitute: I am.

John: Good. I don't want you to think of me as some weird guy that wants to pay you for sex.

You'd better pay her, because she won't sleep with you for kicks.

John: I'd like it if you saw me as a benefactor, helping you through college. Is that how you see me?

Yeah, sure.

Prostitute: Uh, yeah sure.

John: Great. I think this is the best interview I've ever had. OK, now a little about me.

This should be good.

John: I'm married for 17 years. Yea!

Poor broad.

Prostitute: Congratulations.

John: Thanks. I'm pretty happy about it. But our love life has become a little stale.

Prostitute: You don't have to tell me.

The heck he doesn't! Keep talkin', creepy man.

John: I was hoping you could show me the ropes, maybe some new tricks, so I can satisfy my wife in new ways.

Gee whiz, ain't you the sweetest?

Prostitute: That's sweet.

John: Thanks. I like to think so. So, do you think you're up for it? Teaching me positions and stuff? And someday I'll tell my wife about you. I mean, I'm not a bad guy. I did this for her -- and to help you through college. Maybe she'll be into it and want to join a threesome.

Yeah, that's exactly how that conversation will go down.

Prostitute: Maybe.

John: So can we test the engine and take her out for a spin?

Ew-w-w-w-.

Prostitute: Excuse me?

John: Sorry. I just mean, can you prostitute me now?

And they were off.

So next time you're in a coffee shop -- surrounded by writers with their eyes glued to a laptop -- don't jump to judge us. Sure, we may be socially awkward dreamers, believing we are one great script away from buying an island. But we also may be eavesdropping on an epic conversation that we then will write a column about. Maybe even yours. (Insert evil writer cackle here.)

Surprise and the Blue Lion

Children learn about love and the birds and the bees from a variety of places -- parents, guidance counselors, siblings. But I got my first lesson on love and sex from my pet rabbit, Surprise.

I had Surprise for about a year before I brought home a stuffed blue lion I'd just won at the fair. And it was love at first bunny sight. Surprise took one look at the blue lion and had to have her. He hopped over, mounted the blue lion and started to, let's say, vibrate. I didn't know what was happening. Why is my bunny breathing so hard? How is he moving his body so fast? My mom came in and said, "Looks like Surprise is in love." Love? Is this love?

After Surprise lost his virginity to the blue lion, he couldn't be without her. Night and day, he humped her stuffing out. My rabbit wanted that blue lion. He needed that blue lion. He would do his rabbity-duty, and once his heart rate lowered, Surprise would nuzzle his face into the blue lion's mane.

The sexual escapades between Surprise and the blue lion were witnessed frequently by my friends and family. Frankly, they were hard to miss. Eventually, people stopped asking whether I would throw away the ratty old blue lion. They stopped asking whether Surprise was having a heart attack as he wheezed after a good romp. And we all came to accept and embrace their unconventional relationship.

In my opinion, the blue lion had it pretty good, too. No matter how many stuffed animals I offered Surprise to feed his insatiable hunger, he never strayed from his beloved blue lion. He was 100 percent faithful to his beloved. We all should be so lucky.

As the years went on, Surprise's needs became more insatiable. Surprise was caged only when I wasn't home, and he was otherwise free to roam my bedroom. I never separated Surprise from his girlfriend, but once he started doing the deed after dusk -- rattling the cage at all hours -- I started to rethink the living arrangements. I tried training him to make love only during the day, but all my training was in vain. I tried positive reinforcement. I tried negative reinforcement. The results were abysmal. I wonder whether Dr. Pavlov ever tested his behavior conditioning on horny, love-struck rabbits.

One night, in a fit of irritation, I pulled the blue lion out of Surprise's rattling cage and yelled, "You will get her back in a week,

7

when you have learned to control yourself!" Despite his rabbity urges, Surprise remained faithful to the blue lion during their separation. I liked to think that he knew he deserved the punishment.

It wasn't until a week later, when I reunited Surprise with his blue lion, that I realized this relationship was definitely more than just sex. It was love. Surprise immediately mounted the blue lion. He groaned. He moaned. And then, it happened.

The pure jet propulsion of his pent-up week's worth of lovin' was so strong that when Surprise finished, he went flying backward. Flying! I mean, airborne! As he flew backward, Surprise screamed out a kind of "Whoa!" noise that resembled R2-D2's scream after he was electrically shocked in "Episode IV." Surprise flew back more than a foot from the blue lion, hitting his back against my dresser a good 6 inches above the ground. He hit the dresser, fell to the ground, shook it off and hopped away. It was amazing. And I have witnesses.

After Surprise's breathing was back in check, he hopped over to his lady lion and rested his head on hers. He stayed like that, cuddled up, for hours.

I never again took the blue lion away from Surprise. Their love was too great, and the potential for a bunny concussion was too high.

Surprise and the blue lion were in love for six years. When Surprise died, we buried the blue lion with him. I like to think they both would've wanted it that way.

Here's hoping they're humping in rabbit heaven.

Dancing Exotically

"We're very excited by the prospect of having you as a client. Do you have any questions about us and what we do here?"

Staring down at me from behind a huge wooden desk sat a veteran literary agent and my potential new representation. I glanced from her to her teenage-looking assistant, who was bouncing on a yoga ball and jotting down notes. I subconsciously tugged at my pink headband and lace dress, recent purchases made in hopes of creating a youthful appearance for my meeting. By 30, you're practically the Cryptkeeper in my industry. My ultra-adolescent outfit was a pathetic attempt to cover up my granny mothball stench.

"Well, I guess I'm curious whether you are going to give me any extracurricular assignments," I said to the veteran agent.

8

"Of course. We will do our best to get you paid writing assignments."

"No," I said. The veteran agent noticed as I awkwardly pulled on my dress. "I mean more, like, uh, are you going to send me to classes for things outside of my writing ability?"

"I'm not following you," said the veteran.

"I mean, are you going to send me to stripping classes?"

"Excuse me?"

A couple of years ago, my then agent was promoting a script I had written. The story had garnered some interest, and meetings were set up. But one thing was bothering my agent.

"Your story is sexy," she said. "But you -- oh, how do I say this -- aren't."

"They're meeting me because they like my script," I said, "not because they want to sleep with me."

"Oh, I know. But wanting to sleep with you couldn't hurt, right?"

"Uh. I guess not," I said.

"How do you feel about pole dancing?"

Strip-based exercise classes are a big trend in my town. I have no issue with women who take control of their sexuality and their core muscles with some Sunday morning pole dancing. However, I made perfectly clear to my then agent that it was utterly appalling to insist on a client's taking such classes to enhance her sexual appeal in a pitch meeting. There was no way I would partake in that type of blatant, misogynistic, anti-feminist behavior!

A few weeks later, I walked into a brightly lit lobby with floor-to-ceiling shelves of crotchless panties. So much for standing my ground.

I looked down at my baggy T-shirt and yoga pants as the 10 a.m. class let out. Women in their early 60s, wearing sequined corsets, came out of the classroom. They stopped to comment on the newest clothing being sold in the lobby -- specifically the LED-lit Lucite platform high-heeled hooker boots that dazzle like a disco ball every time you take a step and the leather whips -- before continuing on to the changing room.

The classroom was dark, with no windows and no mirrors. Our instructor sat in the center of our circle, yelling out self-affirming statements as we stretched. "Love your womanhood!" "Embrace your Virginia!" I thought about yelling back, "I will once you embrace wearing pants." But I chickened out.

Our warm-up exercise consisted of performing the iconic slinky cat crawl. This required our using our arm and core muscles to lower our upper bodies, barely avoiding sweeping our breasts across the floor, and then pushing our bodies back up as we inched forward on all fours. I was excited to give it a try. I figured, "Hey, I'm here already. May as well make the most of it."

That day, I gained immense respect for my exotic-dancing sisters. Stripping is hard work! I tried to crawl. I tried to slink. I lowered my torso in a suggestive way. But then, just as I was supposed to teasingly lift myself back up, I remembered something: I don't have upper body strength. Bam! My face hit the mat.

The instructor yelled at me to relish my femininity. I tried again. Bam! Face and floor met.

After a few more face plants, I was relegated to the side to watch the other class members slink sexily across the mats. I went home with a bruised ego, an even more bruised nose and nothing new to show my eager husband.

So now, I wasn't ready to go through that embarrassment again.

The veteran agent looked at me, mouth agape. "We would never send you to stripping class."

"Never?"

"With us, you don't even have to dress like a teenager."

Aw, she noticed. I smiled. "Where do I sign?"

~ ~ ~

Chapter 2

Incubation, Gestation and Midsection Inflation: Pregnancy

Baby Names

I begged my parents for a baby. It just wasn't fair! There was nothing in life I wanted more than a younger brother or sister. Reruns of "The Brady Bunch," "The Partridge Family" and "Eight Is Enough" taunted me.

When I was 4, my parents told me there was a baby growing inside my mom's belly. Finally! I screamed, grabbed my mom and said, "Thank you, thank you, thank you!" Because, you know, procreation was obviously on my behalf.

I was obsessed with the creature growing inside my mom. I'd go under the covers and pretend I was going to the mall in my mom's belly; bet you didn't know there was a mall in there! I'd hit up the food court with my incubating little brother and then come out from under the covers and tell my mom everything the fetus and I had discussed. It was all very exciting.

A couple of months before my little brother was born, my parents bestowed the most awesomest of awesome honors upon me: I could pick his middle name.

I obsessed.

To say that I took this honor seriously would be an insult. Naming this unborn child became the sole reason for my existence. I needed a name associated with love. When people heard his middle name, I wanted them to immediately think, "Wow, that little boy is really loved by his big sister." But what name could demonstrate such undying affection and commitment?

I considered the names of boys in my preschool. But all those boys were stupid. No, they wouldn't do.

My mom suggested John.

Lame!

My dad suggested Matthew.

Super-lame!

They suggested Kenneth, Michael, Max, Keith, Tyler, Robert, Patrick...

11

I looked at my parents earnestly and asked, "Why do you hate my little brother?"

I don't remember how it came to me, but one day, I stumbled across the perfect name, a name that would show my little brother just how much his big sister loved him. Friends, family and neighbors would swoon over the careful consideration I had put into naming this unborn child. They would hug me -- cry, even! -- and say, "What a sweet child to give her brother such a name."

I chose the name (drumroll, please) Teddybear.

My mom said, "You mean Ted or Theodore. Right?"

"No, Teddybear. Little girls love their teddy bears. So he'll know I love him."

"Why don't we make his middle name Ted and you can call him Teddybear?"

"No. Teddybear."

"Teddybear isn't a name."

"That's why it's special!"

"Please think of another middle name."

"I did. Teddybear."

I would love to be privy to the conversation my parents must've had after my declaration. Were they bemused? Terrified?

I told my preschool friends about the middle name. *They* loved it.

A month later, my parents woke me up in the middle of the night. Mom was having her baby. A few days after that, I was brimming with excitement as my mom brought home my new best friend, my new partner in crime.

My mom bent down so I could see the baby. I could've fainted from joy.

"This is your new baby brother, Spencer John."

John? John! JOHN!!!

"Um, Mom, you made a mistake. You mean Spencer Teddybear."

"We told you, sweetie, Teddybear isn't a name," my mom said. "Dad and I had said you could pick a *name*."

I was disgusted. I didn't even want to look at the baby. Now he never would know that I was excited about him, that I loved him, so why even try having a relationship? Why bother? I stomped my feet as I marched up the stairs to my bedroom.

My mom yelled after me, "When you have a child of your own, you can name him Teddybear."

"I will!" I screamed defiantly before slamming my bedroom door.

A few months ago, I forwarded the ultrasound picture of my first child to my family.

My little brother, who managed to become my best friend despite his awful middle name, said, "He looks just like a little teddy bear."

He does. But there is no way I'm naming him Teddybear. Turns out that Teddybear is not a name.

Pregnant in a Parking Lot

"People are so nice to you when you're pregnant. They give you the best parking spots. You always get the benefit of the doubt and stock up on free stuff. And you get total permission to act like a crazy, crying freak. You'll see."

To all of my friends who promised I'd find myself sashaying down the lollipop-lined road to maternity, with waving, smiling strangers and a mariachi band intuitively meeting my every need, I have one thing to say to you:

Liars!

Case in point: I recently visited a prenatal clinic during my lunch break. If history had taught me anything, I should've known I was playing with fire. But I'm pregnant. Aren't cars on traffic-jammed highways supposed to part like the Red Sea? Aren't red lights supposed to give me a wink and turn to green just for the heck of it?

Pulling in to the parking lot, I was already running late. I asked the ticket booth operator whether there were any mom-to-be parking spots near the front. He said they were filled. One spot was being used as storage for golf carts. A man on a motorcycle had parked in the other spot.

"Which trimester is the motorcyclist in?" I asked the ticket operator.

He didn't laugh. He just explained that the lot was so full I needed to pull in behind someone and leave my keys in the car in case he needed to move the vehicle.

I parked my Jeep and was in and out of my checkup in 15 minutes. Plenty of time to get back to work. Or so I thought.

Searching for my keys, I quickly realized I'd locked them in my car. Luckily, I own a soft-top Jeep, and (having locked my keys in my car before) I knew all I had to do was unzip the back window, hoist my body up and crawl through. One small hiccup in the plan, though: I wasn't pregnant when I had done this before.

A couple of things became very clear to me very quickly. 1) Hoisting up your body while pregnant is not that easy. 2) Tiny triangular windows are not made for pregnant chicks to squeeze their little meatball bodies through.

I'd never had trouble breaking in to my own car before, but between the lifting and the squeezing, I could not get through the window.

Passers-by on the street stopped and stared. There were no offers of help. There was just staring. A few of them crossed their arms and shook their heads disapprovingly.

"I could use some help," I yelled over to them. "I locked my keys in the car."

"Sure ya did," a guy yelled back. "Enjoy having your baby in jail."

That's when I realized they thought I was breaking in to a stranger's car! Who thinks a pregnant lady would put forth this much effort to steal a car in the middle of the day?! Don't they know we just want to eat and sleep?

Motivated by my need to get back to work and by my fear of cops, I mustered enough energy to hoist my pregnant butt up and through the window. I grabbed the keys off the passenger seat and pulled my Jeep around to the ticket booth, only to find out that I didn't have enough money for my parking ticket.

"I would have enough money, but I was locked out and stuck here for an extra 10 minutes," I explained. The ticket operator didn't care.

I started rummaging through my car, finding any change I could. When I handed over the change, he said: "It's been another five minutes. You owe me another 50 cents."

"But I spent those five minutes looking for change. You watched me do it."

"Another 50 cents."

That's when I started to panic. And by panic, I mean cry. I didn't have the money; I was going to be late for work, and the mean man still was staring at me from across the street, probably laughing at the irony of there being a car thief who couldn't afford to leave the parking lot from which she stole the car.

"Ugh, there's nothing more clichÇd than a pregnant woman crying," said the operator.

I finally got back to work 20 minutes late.

Blanche DuBois may always depend on the kindness of strangers, but that little nut job wasn't preggers.

Lemon Cupcake

"What is that delicious-looking yellow thing?" I asked the barista, my mouth salivating as I pointed to the frosted cone-shaped dessert.

The barista, wearing yoga pants with no intention of actually going to yoga, followed my line of drool.

"It's a lemon cupcake."

"Ooh." I said. "I need that."

She responded with, "Do you?"

I paused a moment, processing what my growing pregnant ears had just heard. Was this woman really mocking me as I tried to patronize her business? The wannabe yogi barista continued.

"I'm just saying, if you're gonna eat that cupcake, maybe you want to work out afterward."

"Are you serious right now?" I asked.

"Hey, don't be mad. I have to work out, too. I'm just saying, maybe a gym membership will do you good."

I should have known this moment was coming. Friends had warned me. Strangers had warned me. The baby books yelled it from the rooftops. Pregnancy is no fun once you have grown a massive gut but don't quite look pregnant. Be warned, the masses cried out. But did I listen? No.

I wasn't concerned. In fact, I was looking forward to packing on the pounds, tipping the scales, breaking chairs when I sat down. It seemed as if it would be a blast. And to be perfectly honest with you, it has been a blast.

I believe that in life, there are times to be thin and there are times to be a chubby bunny. For example, college is a time to chubster it up. You're young, living away from home and eating whatever you want for the first time in your life. Enjoy! I believed in chubby college days so passionately that I gained the freshman 15 both semesters of freshman year. And then again sophomore year just for kicks.

I understand that not everyone shares my views. One beautiful spring day, my college friends and I were chowing down ice cream sundaes when we passed the university's gym and noticed it was packed. There were trails to run, sports to play, friends to see and fun to be had. Why would the gym be packed on a day like today?

As we stood there, pitying the girls running on treadmills on the other side of the window, I spilled chocolate syrup on my shirt. The runner girls laughed. Clearly, they thought we were the ones to be pitied, not the other way around. They pointed at me, whispered to one another and laughed more.

My friends, not ones to be bested, sprang into action. We dug into one another's sundaes and began passing them around, eating them as fast as we could. We rubbed our tummies and yelled out, "Mmm, so good!"

The runner girls stopped laughing. They were not amused.

My friend tapped on the window and offered the runner girls her sundae.

They gave us the bird. We walked away feeling very satisfied.

Maybe I'm lucky; I've always been relatively thin. I believe in being healthy, but not to the point at which it restricts my life. I guess that's why these times of weight fluctuation never bothered me. There are times to be thin, and there are times to be fat.

Pregnancy, to me, is another time to embrace your inner chubby bunny.

So when the wannabe yogi barista questioned my need for a lemon cupcake, I dealt with it the only way I knew how. I ignored her suggestion to get a gym membership, demanded the cupcake and immediately started eating it.

"Mmm. So good," I said, rubbing my tummy. "Want some? Mmm."

I kept up my commentary, making the barista very uncomfortable, until the last bite. Then I licked my fingers and walked out.

Whenever I tell this story, people always ask, "Did you tell her you're pregnant?!"

No, I never mentioned I was pregnant, because to me, that wasn't the point. Pregnant or not, I looked the way I looked.

I was proud of myself, proud that I was above all this nonsense.

That is, until last week, when, for the first time, a stranger asked me my due date.

Proof that I finally looked pregnant. I turned around and startled the stranger by giving her a hug.

Maybe I'm not above it.

Baby Wilson

My kid is kind of a jerk.

Don't freak out; it's what I dig about him. It's how I know the little incubating fetus inside my tummy is mine. And yes, I agree it would be hard for the squirming tyke not to be mine, but still. I've read a lot of Ray Bradbury. Watched enough episodes of "The Twilight Zone." The mind wanders.

Luckily, my fetus has made it easy to squash any science-fiction fears about alien implantation or devil reincarnation. Even in utero, my little spawnster is kind of a jerk, so I know -- undoubtedly, unequivocally -- this kid is mine.

By "jerk," I mean he has spunk. He's stubborn. He likes doing things on his terms.

I mean that he is his mother's son.

When I went in for the first ultrasound, my growing tadpole had a fist covering his nose and mouth. The ultrasound technician started jostling my body, trying to get my incubating fetus to move his hand, but my son-to-be was not having it.

Seeing the disappointment on my face and on my husband's face, the ultrasound technician continued to jostle my bump. She had me lie on one side. Then the other. With each jostle, my son-to-be covered his face a little more, slowly crossing both his arms in front of him. His two little fists covered his face as much as they could. The technician began tapping on my stomach. Almost hitting it. My son-to-be responded by spreading out his fingers. Optimal face coverage. The technician gave up.

One point baby-to-be. Zero points mommy-to-be.

I was bummed that I couldn't see my full baby but told myself that there was a lesson to be learned here. What was it? Patience? Let sleeping fetuses lie? I settled on feeling grateful that my kid was in such good health that the technician could waste her time on something as trivial as trying to get a good picture so I could show friends and family.

My husband and I started calling the baby Wilson after the next-door neighbor in the sitcom "Home Improvement." You never saw his nose or mouth, either.

Every ultrasound since has followed the exact same pattern. My little spawnster's nose and mouth are covered from the get-go. The more we harass him the more he hides. He nestles his face in the placenta. Covers his face with his arms. And, without fail, the technician gives up, and I get sent home without a picture of my growing baby's face.

See? The kid is a brat. And I love that about him. I love that he is stubborn. I love that he insists on living by his own rules.

Am I applying personality attributes to a not-yet-person that are completely fabricated and may have nothing to do with the person my son will become?

Absolutely.

But pregnancy is an odd time -- a time when you are trying to connect with someone you never have met. His perceived bratty and stubborn behavior makes him someone I know, someone I recognize. It makes him a mini-me.

Our silly little spawnster's antics also have helped my husband become more emotionally connected to him. They say daddies-to-be have a hard time connecting to their babies while they are still in utero. How can you feel attached when it isn't your body that's changing? And my husband, like many, felt slightly as if he were benched for the big game -- that is, until one of our ultrasounds, during which our son kept his legs perfectly crossed and dignified as he continued to hide his face from the technician. My husband proudly stated: "He's a mix of both of us! He's dignified like me and a brat like you!"

My son can be whoever he wants to be when he arrives. But until he can decide for himself who that person is, we are having fun finding ourselves in his fetal actions.

Today I went in for another ultrasound. But this time, my little man must've sensed that I needed to have the visual confirmation of not just his eyes and ears but also his nose and mouth. For a brief moment, he lowered his arms and yawned. Proof he has a mouth! My son-to-be then promptly placed his hands back over his face.

"Ugh, this kid is so stubborn," the ultrasound technician said.

Yep, that's my boy.

Zombie Baby

When two of my good friends got married last year, I bought them both books on the topics that were occupying their minds most. For the baby-crazed bride-to-be, there was "What to Expect When You're Expecting," and for the groom, I selected a zombie survival guide. Naturally.

A few months later, my friends and I found ourselves spread out in my backyard, surrounded by zombie manuals and baby guides, working on a book that combined both of their interests: "What to Expect When You're Expecting a Zombaby." (Working title.)

We structured the zombaby book just like all the other pregnancy books we had scattered around us -- taking the reader from conception to all the stages of the pregnancy and zom-mom care to delivery and care for the zombaby. Here are a few of the chapters:

--Conception. You've had a one-night stand with a zombie. Now what? How to cope when you know he is going to be a DEADbeat dad.

--Choosing your doctor and hospital. Picking a specialist with a zombaby ward. Inexperienced doctors have lost fingers while administering pelvic exams to zom-moms.

--The changing body of the zom-mom. Rather than have the typical pregnancy glow, a zom-mom will develop an ashen complexion, will have bags under her eyes and will grow stronger teeth to rip apart the raw meat she'll crave. She also may develop a tendency to sleepwalk with her arms outstretched.

--Cravings. That's not your stomach growling; that's your zombaby making his presence known. Soothe the little guy by drinking embalming fluids and formaldehyde. (Stop activity immediately after birth of zombaby.)

--Sexual activity. Zom-moms-to-be experience mantis-type tendencies. Try not to fornicate with anyone you care about during your zombaby's gestation. You might accidentally bite off your partner's head. Literally.

--Exercise. Heavy emphasis on the cardio. After your li'l zombaby is born, you will spend a lot of time running for your life.

--Life insurance vs. death insurance.

--Delivery. Your zombaby will claw and bite his way out. Make sure the nurses are ready with leather gloves, a crate and a plate of raw meat.

--Breast-feeding. Don't!

--Socialization/angry mobs. Friends don't let friends pitchfork each other's baby.

And there are many more.

We finished the book and turned it into a screenplay. It is a fun little script, slapstick and absurd, and obviously has no truth to it.

Or so I thought.

I was flipping through the pages of a few pregnancy books recently -- actually reading them to learn about my incubating fetus, not to bastardize them into yet another zombie survival guide -- and do you know what I realized?

I think I'm pregnant with a zombaby!

First of all, it turns out my baby literally is eating my brain. Did you know that? Because I sure as heck didn't. Apparently, MRI scans have proved that your brain shrinks during pregnancy. No one seems to know exactly why that is, but one theory is that during pregnancy, your fetus essentially feeds on your fat storage, and our brains are pretty darn fatty. If this isn't proof that I'm pregnant with a zombaby, I don't know what is.

Need further disturbing proof? Did you know that during gestation, pregnant women double the amount of blood pumping through them? Now, I agree that excess blood supply seems to be more of a vampirebaby trait, but it still doesn't make me feel all warm and fuzzy inside.

Zombies are monosyllabic. I don't exactly expect my little guy to come out with an advanced vocabulary. I assume he will just cry and moan to communicate, just as the zombies do.

Zombies rise out from damp, dark places -- kind of like the way my baby will.

Zombies feast off humans. I intend on breast-feeding.

Do you see the similarities, people?!

And for just one second, can we all admit that I've got something moving inside me -- making his presence known quite well -- but not breathing! C'mon, are we all really going to pretend that isn't the tiniest bit creepy?

But don't worry; I still love my little zombaby.

Now I'll have to find a way to tell my husband about my drunken night in Cabo with a zombie.

The Baby-CPR Monster

"Baby, wake up! Oh, no! Somebody help my baby! Please!"

Don't worry; I'm not quoting a real parent in distress. Rather, I am quoting my over-the-top, insane, crazy-pants baby-CPR instructor.

Living in Los Angeles, you are surrounded by folks who work one job but wish they were working in the Hollywood industry instead. Sure, your waiter is taking auditions by day, but it's so much more than that. The grocers are animators; the bank tellers are editors; and what the dentists really want to do is direct. So I don't know why I was thrown off-guard when my instructor turned our class about how to give CPR to a baby into an audience for her one-man show.

The baby CPR class was the last in a series of classes my husband and I were taking to prepare us for childbirth and baby care. The classes had been stellar, but this particular class was different from the get-go. For starters, each person got his own CPR Chucky doll to play with. The dolls had holes in their mouths to breathe into and chest cavities that rose and fell. OK, they didn't exactly look like Chucky per se, but there was something about these dolls that made you instinctively know that if the lights were turned off, their heads would start spinning.

Then there was the teacher. She seemed so normal at first. A woman in her late 50s, she spoke softly and kindly and walked us through what to do if we found our babies not breathing and unresponsive. She delicately instructed us to tap our babies' feet and say, "Baby, wake up." Then she taught us to examine the baby, waiting 10 seconds to see whether he breathes before starting chest compressions. She demonstrated how to place two fingers at the center of the baby's chest, just below the nipple line, and press down 30 times to the beat of "Stayin' Alive." And lastly, she showed us how to tilt the baby's head back, looking for objects in his mouth, before breathing into it twice and repeating the chest compressions.

Then it was our turn to practice.

We began tapping our dolls' feet, asking them to wake up.

"Like you mean it!" the CPR instructor yelled. Everyone looked up at her, startled by the outburst from this seemingly sweet lady.

The monster had been unleashed.

"Like this." She screamed over us, "Baby, baby, wake up! Oh, God! Please, baby!"

The bewildered eyes of my fellow classmates darted across the room as if to ask, "The instructor realizes she's talking to a doll, right?"

It didn't matter how loudly we yelled; the doll wasn't going to wake up. Then again, these Chucky dolls just might've. But to me, all the less reason to disturb them!

"OK, class, now what?" the CPR instructor asked.

The class began examining the dolls as we timidly counted to 10 aloud, but our voices were drowned out. Our instructor enhanced her one-man show by crying over the dolls. Literally crying.

"Oh, gosh! Why me?" The CPR instructor wailed. "Why my baby? Why?"

Don't worry; I don't believe her tears stem from any real trauma. The waterworks were turned on and off too quickly; the theatrics were too absurd.

The instructor then had us practice our chest compressions and breathing as she continued to cry on cue and yell at the inanimate dolls to wake up. When she decided we had successfully brought the dolls back to life, crazy CPR lady made baby crying noises. But I don't mean she just said "wha" a couple of times. That would be reasonable! No, she held the cry for a good 30 seconds as, again, our class looked around in silent wonder. Was this crackpot for real?

When she had completed her baby-brought-back-from-the-dead performance, the instructor asked, "Is your baby alive?"

Beyond agitated, a guy in the back yelled out, "No!"

We repeated the exercise numerous times as the instructor continued to yell and cry over us.

When class had ended, she handed out her card. I'm shocked it wasn't a headshot.

The 30 of us shuffled out of the classroom, exhausted by the insanely odd four-hour dramatic interpretation of a parent in crisis.

That being said, I clearly remember each CPR step I was taught in my bizarre class, and that's by far the most important thing. Maybe crazy CPR lady wasn't so crazy after all. Then again...

That Evil Temptress Sleep

Sleep, you elusive siren you. Why do you mock me so?

I wish I could fall asleep easily. It sounds lovely. But alas, sleep and I have never seen eye to eye on the issue. I want a relationship with sleep, but sleep wants to keep seeing other people.

The slut.

I can't really blame sleep for not making a commitment to me. I haven't exactly been the best suitor. Even after my head hits the pillow and I beckon sleep to adventure to dream world with me, I wind up lying awake for hours. I promise her travel and leave her stranded at the gate.

I blame my parents. It was often overheard in my household growing up, "It's almost midnight? Why aren't the kids in their rooms yet?" My parents would take turns saying this to each other, both equally shocked that yet again, a responsible bedtime had evaded them. Naps were just as passionately enforced.

Sleep and I were never close -- second cousins at best. But in the past nine months, sleep and I have gone from cool acquaintances to full-on frienemies.

My desire for sleep has grown quite drastically in this second half of my pregnancy, but we are not closer or more intimate. If anything, I think sleep has taken this opportunity to become a bit of a tease. She dances around me -- controlling me, making promises she won't keep -- and then comes knocking at the most inconvenient of times.

Rather than let me experience the relationship most other pregnant women have with sleep -- feeling tired in the early stages of pregnancy and then becoming an insomniac near the end -- sleep decided to mess with my head from the start. She made me simultaneously an insomniac and a narcoleptic.

I try to reconcile with sleep. Overwhelmed by fatigue, I get under my covers each night at a reasonable hour, but my exhaustion does not bring on that cruel temptress. Rather, she takes her sweet time to arrive -- primping her hair, I assume -- visits for only an hour or two and then disappears, leaving me wanting more. Needing more.

I've tried to nourish my body with naps. Attempting to seduce sleep, I take a bath with calming oils, listen to soft music, put on my favorite pajamas and crawl under the covers. But sleep deletes my calls.

And in the cruelest twist of all, sleep won't entirely let me go. She will pop up unexpectedly, keeping me holding on to hope, wishing for a day we could be together like a normal couple. Her random stopovers have turned me into a narcoleptic.

Throughout this pregnancy, I have not been able to sleep properly, but I have managed to pass out everywhere. And I mean everywhere.

I was taking the trash out at my work and woke up on the stoop in the back alley behind my building. I don't remember sitting down on the stoop, let alone putting my head down on the garbage-covered concrete. When I came back in, my co-workers said I had been gone for about 40 minutes. Oops.

Then there was that time I went to pick up Chinese food. I remember passing the homeless man who always sits outside the restaurant as I went in to place the order. The next thing I remember is waking up on the bench, with the homeless man glaring down at me.

"You're in my spot," he said. He is "The Big Bang Theory's" Sheldon Cooper of homeless men.

I've fallen asleep in my car, at park tables, on the floor at work, on my driveway -- never with the intention or desire to actually fall asleep at that moment.

My affinity for resting my eyes in back alleys probably isn't the safest or wisest move for a pregnant lady. I think it's time I swallow my pride and apologize to sleep for whatever I've done to upset her so. What kind of flowers does sleep like?

I hope sleep and I can resume our old relationship. It wasn't perfect, but at least after a few hours of her holding out, she usually would let me slumber until my morning alarm. Please, dearest sleep, no more waking me a million times throughout the night. No more narcolepsy throughout the day.

I'm sure this is just a phase, a blip in the relationship. Sleeping should be much easier once the baby gets here, right?

Hello?

Granny's Induction Home Remedies

There's a reason women have come up with so many crazy home remedies to induce labor: Being nine months pregnant is terrible.

If my experience speaks to most women's at nine months, waiting for your child to enter this world is maddening. You become a crazy person -- even crazier than the hormones have made you thus far. Every day, you find yourself praying for an end to come soon. Every day, you look for signs, hoping today is the day.

Are those contractions or just stomach pains from drinking milk past its expiration date? Did my water just break, or did I just laugh too hard? Did my awesome dream about bathing in a pool of Bisquick and lying out in the sun chanting "I'm a delicious pig in a blanket" indicate that I soon will be holding my own li'l bundle in a blanket? (Oh, come on! I can't be the only person who had that dream.)

You know the truth. You know that it's simply time to avoid Comedy Central and seek out a restaurant serving mini dough-covered hot dogs before that unfortunate bout of food poisoning knocks you on your rear. But still, you hold on to hope. Maybe today I will get to meet my child.

And when simply hoping isn't enough and desperation seeps in, ladies in my position visit Granny's old home remedy recipe box.

There are many home remedies that claim to dilate your cervix, cause contractions and induce labor. Just a few days out from my due date, I decided it was time to start exploring Grandma's old induction secrets.

--Castor oil. Perhaps Nana's most popular and well-known home remedy is drinking castor oil. And from what I understand, the baby may be vacating himself from his mother's womb simply to escape its wretched taste as it filters through the umbilical cord. Some women take this foul-tasting oil mixed with orange juice or chased with ginger ale. Those lucky ladies who haven't already grown their fair share of hair on their chest from the hormones may opt to take the castor oil plain. My limited research into Nana's castor oil solution indicates that the oil irritates your bowels and can create a domino effect that eventually leads to uterine contractions. In addition to the awful taste, the oil can give your baby a case of the runs while he's still inside you. Thanks but no thanks, Grandma. Next!

--Coffee trick. Another favorite of Granny's secret home remedies is lovingly referred to as the coffee trick. To perform this absurd induction remedy, the mother-to-be must fill a bowl with a cup of freshly ground coffee beans and boiling water. She then places the bowl into the toilet and lets it float on the toilet water. Lastly, big ol' Preggers is supposed to sit her tuchis down on the seat and let the caffeinated steam toast up her nether region. I know that women do a lot of strange and crazy things to their special area -- read: Brazilian waxes -- but getting a third-degree burn is not on my to-do list. Next!

--Sex. Ha-ha, that's adorable. Next!

I was starting to lose hope. The spicy food remedy gave me heartburn. The pineapple remedy made me nauseated. Would I ever find a labor-inducing remedy that appealed to me? C'mon, Nana, help a top-heavy sister out! And that's when I heard about the labor cake.

Cue clouds parting, sunbeams shining and angels singing.

--Labor cake. Labor cake is the tastiest bit of propaganda I've ever heard of. Whosoever nana dreamed up this little ditty deserves a hug and a government job. Here's the brilliant recipe: Buy a box of devil's-food cake, and follow the directions. In addition to the regular mix-in ingredients, add a cup of sour cream, 2 cups of chocolate pudding and a bag of chocolate morsels. Voila! Labor cake. Of all the induction secrets I read up on, this one seems to have worked the least, but nine months in, with swollen feet and broken spirits, don't we mamas-to-be deserve a little sugar shock while we play out this waiting game? I think so.

The oven is preheating, and I'm heading to the store as soon as I submit this column.

Oh, Grandma's induction remedy, you may not work, but you will be delicious.

The Nice Man With the Big Scary Needle

I don't care if your middle name is Kumbaya; the car ride to labor and delivery is anxiety-inducing. A million fears bubble to the surface -- fears you have been actively suppressing for nine months, fears that you know are irrational but can't help obsessing over.

What if my baby's cone head never goes back down? Will I have to learn French and pray he has the same facial features and comedic timing of Dan Aykroyd? What if that purple goo never washes off him? Will he have the right number of fingers and toes? I only know of one six-fingered man, and he killed Inigo Montoya's father. What if the murder gene resides in my child's misplaced sixth finger?

And then, of course, there are the real fears -- the ones that are in the back of every pregnant woman's mind, the ones too scary to write down even now.

The teachers in my mommy-prep classes would ask us ladies whether we had any fears. No one talked about the cone head anxiety or those terrifying unmentionables. Rather, the No. 1 fear mentioned, without fail, was of the epidural.

I assumed most of these mommies-to-be feared the nice man with the big scary needle because it was something tangible to wrap their other, more devastating fears into -- projecting their nervous energy into a fear they could cope with.

I was not like these women. I had been able to keep my fears at bay without funneling them into something like the epidural. That is, until the car ride, when I, too, joined the bandwagon of trypanophobics. I tried calming myself down, telling myself it was silly to fear a needle, even a python-sized one.

I was wrong.

The not-so-nice man with the big needle was called in to administer my epidural once my contractions were coming two minutes apart. Without warning, he plunged the monstrous syringe into my spine. I screamed out in pain. But it wasn't my back that killed; it was my left hip.

"Why would your hip hurt?" the anesthesiologist snapped.

I wanted to scream, "I don't know, man! You're the doctor!" But then I remembered he was holding a stake. Best not to tick him off.

Dr. Happy looked for a place to stab me. Again. In went the needle. I screamed from the pain in my hip. Out came the needle.

We did this little dance for 20 agonizing minutes.

After the anesthesiologist finally successfully laced into my back the IV tube that would administer my drugs, he said, "I don't appreciate that you took me double the time it usually takes."

Yeah, well, it was no picnic for me, either, bub!

I never wanted to see Dr. Friendly again, but an hour later, I still was flailing from side to side, crying out, "Why aren't the drugs working?"

Dr. Sparklepants eventually re-entered and insisted that the drugs were working and that I was being a big baby. He reluctantly administered another bump to my epidural before leaving the room.

I still didn't feel any relief. I thrashed around until a nurse noticed that my IV had been pulled out from all my squirming.

"Well, you need that IV in ya if you wanna feel somethin', honey," the nurse said, sticking the IV back in. Ah, instant relief -- to the left side of my body.

The nurses laid me on my right side, hoping gravity would correct Dr. Smile's failings. But before the right side of my body could go numb, it was time to push. The next thing I knew, I was looking into my son's eyes.

They say women don't remember the pain of childbirth, because if we did, we'd be too afraid to do it again. I don't remember much of the pain from pushing, but I can tell you what I do remember.

I remember pulling my crying baby up onto my chest. I remember feeling surprised that in that moment, I was not afraid. I didn't care about his cone head. I didn't care that he was covered in purple slime. I didn't count his fingers and toes. I wasn't afraid of the unmentionables, because in that moment, he was perfect.

The ladies were right to place all their fears into the big needle. There is no point in worrying about things you can't control, especially when the odds are that your baby will come out perfect and healthy as mine did. The epidural, however, is another story.

~ ~ ~

Chapter 3

How Early Is Too Early to Give Your Baby an "I <3 Mom" Tattoo?: Parenting

A Letter to My Newborn Son

Sweet Baby,

I promise always to be your biggest cheerleader, even during that weird phase when you're into wearing a cape and playing the electric cello.

I promise I won't pretend to understand current fashion trends when you're in school. Be it turtlenecks made of banana peels or a resurgence of parachute pants and monocles, you're free to dress as you choose, as long as it doesn't represent the Bloods, the Crips or any of the 50 shades of gray.

I hope you will have enough self-worth never to be an easy victim and enough character never to be a bully. Only comfort in your own skin will bring you real joy in life. Well, that and chocolate-covered bacon.

I promise never to act as if my love were something you must earn. There will be days when I won't like you very much, my sweet, but my love for you is constant. It's a right, not a privilege. It's yours with my every breath until my last breath and beyond.

I hope you take yourself seriously but never take life too seriously. Approach life with a sense of humor, and have sense enough to know when to use it and when to shut your mouth. Only Joe Biden can laugh in a guy's face for an hour and not get decked.

Be warned: I sing off key and loudly, stick my foot in my mouth, always raise my hand when a magician asks for a volunteer, walk into walls and tell absurd stories to strangers who didn't ask to hear them. But though I'm likely to embarrass you often, I promise never to shame you.

I promise to apologize when I've erred, because it is important you know that there is great strength and grace in saying "I'm sorry" and meaning it.

I hope you go through a rebellious phase, when you stake your independence and claim your own voice, even if that means a tongue ring and a misspelled gangsta pseudonym, such as Kla$$ Klown.

And I am putting this in writing so you can shove it in my face when I deny ever permitting such insolence.

I promise never to chaperone your school dances.

I hope you always will come to me with the big issues. But I pray those big issues look less like an episode of "16 and Pregnant" and more like an episode of "What Not to Wear."

I promise never to lie to you. However, I reserve the right to stretch the truth, omit information, be hyperbolic and change names to protect the guilty.

I hope you are always up for learning. Please, please, my child, we have enough morons in this world.

I hope you always run down hills with outstretched arms, wish on dandelions, play with slugs, jump in puddles and climb trees far too high.

I hope life hands you a few big falls, but none so serious that it can't be remedied with a little humility or a couple of months in a neon cast signed by all your friends.

I wish for you passion and the guts to pursue it. Though I reserve the right to retract this statement if your passion leads you to a life of selling drugs, porn or jumping out of planes in nothing but a squirrel suit. Them folks be crazy.

I hope you are a brat -- not in the spoiled way but in the "I've got my own mind and I'm not afraid to speak it" way. Brats can change the world.

And most of all, I hope your never feel small when you stand beside the ocean -- or the mountains or the desert, for that matter. I hope you feel huge. There is nothing insignificant about you, little one. You have but one life, and this earth is yours to swim and climb and trek. It is yours to explore and to protect. Stop for the sunsets, and count the stars; and when the world opens up to show you her magnificence, feel huge because you got to see it. And because you were here, breathing her air, this world never will be the same again. You have impacted the planets, my love. That's how special you are, my big boy. That's how grand.

My heart is yours,
Mommy

The Unintentional Nudist

I've become an exhibitionist.

It's not my fault; I don't mean to be flashing the goods. If anything, I'm a prude. But lately, I haven't seemed to have my wits about me. Or my shirt.

My downward spiral into accidental nudism began a little more than a year ago. It all started innocently enough. I was cleaning the bathroom and opened a window protected by my security system, thus accidentally setting off the alarm. No worries. I quickly punched in the code on my security system and continued cleaning. Seeing as I was working with bleach and intended on taking a shower after I spiffed up the toilet, I was cleaning in the nude. Who cares, right? I'm in my house. The open window faced my backyard. I shouldn't feel ashamed about being nude in my own bathroom! And I didn't. That is, until the police officer, alerted by the security company, stuck his head in my open bathroom window.

"Ma'am?"

"Oh, my gosh, you scared me!" I screamed.

"No one answered your door. I need you to come around front and let me in," the officer said. "And, miss, you may want to throw a shirt on."

Color me crimson. Who knew cleaning the shower was a gateway drug to the nudist lifestyle? Be careful to avoid my fate, friends, and consider hiring a cleaning person. Once the fuzz saw my fanny, there was no turning back.

This past spring and summer, I was pregnant and then super-pregnant. The staggering heat outside combined with the incubating-baby heat inside created a lethal combination. That is, a lethal combination for my clothes. Oh, sure, they claimed to be lightweight, but they were never light enough. One hundred percent cotton, nylon and poly-blends be damned. I tried to stay decent. I spent the later months of my pregnancy walking around my house in my undergarments, fighting the urge to disrobe completely. But as the temperature soared into the triple digits and my air conditioner broke, even the undergarments lost their battle.

So what? My nudity was my business and no one else's. And it would've stayed my business if my husband didn't have an annoying habit of opening the blinds every morning. To be honest, it's not his fault. There is a kind of apathy that takes over in the later months of pregnancy. And with my air conditioner broken and my baby baking for a couple of more months, I left those windows wide-open. On the plus side, dog walkers and runners got an added incentive to hit the pavement. Then again, at eight months pregnant, maybe my naked body was more of a deterrent.

Luckily, my foray into baring it all had remained behind walls. Oh, sure, there was that year when I was living in Australia and my girlfriends and I thought we would brave sunbathing topless at a nude beach. The extreme sunburn that followed is one that I wouldn't wish on my worst enemy. For a week, I wore suspenders with chopsticks horizontally duct-taped on them under my loosest shirts to keep the cloth from touching my tatas. It was a blast having to explain that fashion choice to my friends and teachers.

But that was Australia! It doesn't count. I was just indulging in local culture. When in Rome, right? Here, in the good ol' US of A, I act like a proper daughter of our Puritanical heritage. I'm fairly certain that if you play "The Star-Spangled Banner" backward, you will hear this chant: Be prude, not nude. I followed that credo. I believed in it. Even when a dirty bathroom and a summer pregnancy sent me spiraling, I was sure to only wear my birthday suit indoors. That is, until this past weekend.

I had just finished breast-feeding my son, when I realized I had left his diaper bag in my car. I headed out to my vehicle parked a few houses away, waving hello to neighbors I had finally spoken to just a few nights before while trick-or-treating. The neighbors seemed a bit reserved but waved back at me. It wasn't until I re-entered my home and felt the cooled air on my bare stomach that I looked down at my body panic-stricken. What had I done?

My husband walked by, smiled and said, "Next time, you may want to throw a shirt on."

Words to live by.

Chrismukkah Cheer

All of these stupid holiday cards are really starting to get me peeved.

Growing up, I celebrated both Hanukkah and Christmas. December used to be a month of joy -- a month of storytelling and charity, of hot meals and endless presents, of chocolate in the shape of gold coins and in steamy cups with marshmallows. December used to be my favorite month.

But now December mocks me.

It turns out that though I was the gleeful recipient of holiday cheer, I'm not so great at creating it. And with every dang holiday card that enters my mailbox, December shames my holiday ineptitude all the more.

Two days after Thanksgiving, I received my first generic holiday card from one of those 12-packs you buy at the local pharmacy. If all the cards I've been sent had remained so impersonal, I might still be able to look at myself in the mirror. But no-o-o. My loved ones insisted on wallpapering my mailbox with pictures of their smiling families and personalized notes. The jerks!

I even received one homemade holiday card from a friend who included a page-length update on 2012 and a picture of her four kids (all younger than 6). As if that weren't enough, the card sat in a pillow of homemade fake snow. Snow! I mean, c'mon! Is she trying to make me drown my shame in a bottle of Manischewitz?

I get it, people! You're all goddesses of time management. Maybe Father Time has magically bent the rules of the 24-hour day for you eggnog-drinking, brisket-broiling senders of holiday cards, but I still am working within the normal Earth spin cycle. And 24 hours just isn't enough.

It's not just the holiday cards that shame me. It's the parties. And the gift exchanges. And the lights. Good grief, the lights! We were never allowed to put up Christmas lights when I was a kid. I vowed that when I became an adult, I would string Christmas lights a la Clark Griswold. I wouldn't stop until I caused a citywide power outage. But now I can't fathom when I'd find the free time to attempt such a lofty endeavor. So naturally, my neighbor across the street is living out my childhood dream, complete with spelling out "Merry Christmas" in lights across his front lawn. I hate him.

Don't you people have jobs? And families? And shopping to do? How do you find enough hours in the day?

Every night this week, I stared at the box of matzo ball soup in my pantry. I considered taking an hour to bring Hanukkah into my home. Then my baby would cry, and I would grab a frozen dinner instead.

And I was OK with that. I'd come to terms with my holiday dispirit. Or, I would have come to terms with it if my fanatical friends would let me. Though it certainly was not ideal that I couldn't work into my schedule a rendezvous between my 3-month-old and the mall Santa, I wasn't losing sleep over it. My friend, however, wouldn't hear of such a thing. Two days after I kvetched about my tight schedule, he showed up at my house dressed like the big man in red -- twinkle in eye and belly full of jelly in tow.

Do you see the kind of holiday extremists I'm working with? Every kindhearted gesture shamefully reminds me that I'm doing nothing to bring in the season.

Yesterday I was weighing whether a tree was even necessary, when the news anchorman on my television announced that this year's Christmas trend is to have multiple trees. I laughed, fairly certain the universe was just sticking it to me. Message received. Santa's shame game got me off my tuchis and into a Christmas tree lot.

My little family picked a 6-foot grand fir. We even found time to take it off the roof of the car. I got out my ornaments and menorahs from the garage and decorated my living room with holiday cheer. My husband and I toasted spiced wine as our son's eyes transfixed on the Hanukkah candles. From the outside, I still look like a Grinch. But inside, my home is pungent from pine. There is chocolate in the shape of gold coins and in steamy cups with marshmallows.

It's starting to look a lot like Chrismukkah.

I'd send you a picture, but heaven knows I'm not doing holiday cards this year.

Conversations at the Pump

"Can you sign for this package?" asked the UPS deliveryman as he handed a large package through my car window to where I sat. I made no movement to take the package.

"Just bring it inside." I nodded to the back door of my office, where the deliveries usually are made.

"Oh, c'mon, Did. I'm swamped. Just take the package," he pleaded.

"I'm a little busy right now, Roger," I said, still making no motion to pick up the package.

"Just do me this favor. What's the big deal?"

"The big deal," I said, "is that my hands are a little busy right now holding suction cups to my boobs!"

Roger pulled the package back out from my window, averting his eyes, as if he suddenly were granted the gift of X-ray vision and could miraculously see through the blanket that was covering both me and my breast pump.

I pump breast milk in my car. My office doesn't have a suitable place to pump, so twice a day, I head out to my parking spot at work. I turn on the car battery, plug in my pump, lower the window so I don't die from fumes and pump for 15 minutes.

Over the years, there have to have been a thousand times when I've sat alone in my car with the window down. I swear, up until I attached a machine to my breasts, those moments of privacy always remained private. But now that I have the super-fun daily task of getting hooked up to an alien-esque contraption, every Tom, Dick and Harry wants to yell over the crunching noise of the pump and chat.

Co-workers have leaned their heads through my window and started up conversations without a moment's hesitation. I had a stranger do the same, inquiring whether my car was for sale. Once, a woman opened my door, attempting to forcibly recruit me into finding her runaway dog. And some kid asked me whether he could bum a cigarette. When I told him I don't smoke, he kicked my tires. I considered running after the teenage twerp, but what could I do, threaten to squirt milk in his eye? My breasts aren't Super Soakers, and if they were, I wouldn't have to be hooked up to such a God-awful machine.

My friend Marco says this bizarre attention is caused by a subconscious magnetic attraction to a breast-feeding mammal. "It's biology," he said. "They can sniff you out. No one knows you're breast pumping. They just know they have a desire to talk to you."

This premise is a little disconcerting. What if I'm a culprit, too, and all the women I find myself randomly engaging in conversation with are secretly pumping like me? Any woman sitting alone and wearing a blanket or oversize clothing is now suspect. I always have wanted to carry on a conversation with Judge Judy, and who knows what she's hiding under those robes?!

The sudden influx of Chatty Cathys has been so irritating because trying to feed your child only breast milk when you are a working mom is hard enough as it is. I actively have to work on keeping up my milk supply. I hydrate all day, and it's never I enough. I add flaxseed and brewer's yeast to nearly everything I eat. And let me tell you, those ingredients are not known for being flavor enhancers. I drink a lactation enhancement tea that makes me smell so much like syrup that I could be mistaken for Mrs. Butterworth. Give it another month and truckers will pull off the highway, thinking my office is a Waffle House.

I hate pumping. And conversations at the pump are the worst. The only awesome thing about pumping at work is that twice a day, I get a 15-minute break. And as a sleep-deprived mom, that's something I cherish.

A couple of weeks ago, I was in my car, battery running, window down, taking my pumping break, and for the first time in a very long time, no one harassed me. No stranger came to my window or even made eye contact while walking by. I was just about to think that my personal pump station on wheels wasn't so bad, when my car battery died.

I needed a jump because of the pump. I could've used a friendly stranger -- one with jumper cables.

Steps, Stumbles and Seasoned Parenting

There is a special kind of horror reserved for the first time you watch your child fall, face-first, off an elevated surface. (Let me reassure you that my son was fine. I wasn't, but my son was.)

Out of sheer guilt, I've spent the past week telling everybody I know about my mothering mishap -- that I, someone with the nerve to call herself a parent, allowed my only child to plunge off a couch. A good 18 inches, mind you. That's, like, 46 centimeters! It's 457 millimeters!

I wanted to be punished, scolded. Call protective services! Someone, please. For the good of humanity!

But instead, all I got were knowing nods, empathetic grins and supportive comments of parenting camaraderie, such as, "Yeah, kids'll do that."

Kids'll do that?

"Oh, really?" I blew up at one of my friends. "Are we speaking in general terms now? Do all kids -- of every race, religion and socio-economic status -- systematically stumble from raised surfaces the moment their parents' backs are turned?"

"Yes." She simply said yes.

And that's when I realized where I had erred. I had been seeking shaming tongue-lashings from seasoned parents. Seasoned parents!

You know the type -- those relaxed, self-assured people. Survivors of the child rearing rodeo. They make me sick with their confidence and all their knowing of stuff.

A few days ago, I was at my son's day care facility and witnessed one of the older kids fall from the monkey bars. The difference in the parenting style of that child's seasoned parent compared with my new parenting tactic was shocking. Both seasoned parents and the new parents take clear steps to address their crying child, but the approach to these steps is -- well, let's just say different:

--Step 1. Seasoned parent: Calls out "you're OK" to the crying child after a stumble.

New parent: Runs to the fallen baby, scoops him up and checks to see whether the baby is dead, ignoring the screaming, the tears and all other obvious signs that the child is quite certainly alive. Considers administering CPR but is unable to get close enough as the baby swats at the parent's face.

--Step 2. Seasoned parent: Asks the still-crying child, "Did the fall frighten you?"

New parent: Reels with agonizing guilt after realizing that she lifted the baby. Doing that after a neck or spine injury would paralyze the child. Immediately starts slapping baby's feet to make sure they move. They do.

--Step 3. Seasoned parent: If the child still is crying, the parent gets up and walks over to check for injuries. "Do you have a scratch?"

New parent: "Do you have a concussion?" Checks for eye dilation and skull contusions as she waits for the doctor to return her call. Considers whether she would move closer to family if she discovered her child just suffered brain damage.

--Step 4. Seasoned parent: "Show me where it hurts." The kid points, and the parent applies soft pressure to the spot to gauge how bad the injury really is.

New parent: Hangs up the phone after the doctor reassures her that her baby is fine. Immediately decides doctor is a moron. Methodically applies soft pressure to every inch of the baby's body to check for broken bones while making a mental log of friends she can ask for new pediatrician recommendations.

--Step 5. Seasoned parent: Ascertains the severity of the injury. Makes a diagnosis and -- assuming it's not an emergency -- gives a great big hug and a kiss.

New parent: Finally becomes fairly convinced that her child is not on death's door. Ascertains the true severity of the injury. Makes a diagnosis and -- assuming it's not an emergency -- gives a great big hug and a kiss.

On Step 5, the kid at my day care stopped wailing. On Step 5, my baby had stopped wailing, too. The seasoned day care mom plowed through her five steps in about 60 seconds. My five steps took about 15 minutes and at least three years off my life. The day care mom walked away from the situation with a smile on her face, unfazed. I have 20 new gray hairs and still feel ready to break into tears.

I'm looking forward to becoming a seasoned parent. If I keep this up, I'll go through every pediatrician in the Western Hemisphere before my child turns 2.

A Mall Mecca

"This place is sweet!"

My husband ran his fingers along the sleek furniture, admiring the stylish pad. It was as if we had stumbled onto something magical, like Alice tripping through the looking glass and winding up in a world of wonder that, though unimaginable, was somehow built as if with her in mind. My husband was right. This place was totally sweet. The sweetest bathroom there ever was.

Not so much a bathroom, per se, as a Family Changing Station. You wouldn't call an Aston Martin a *car*, would you? What we had here was a bona fide 20-by-20-foot sanctuary of mahogany paneling, intoxicating airflow of island breeze Febreze and the wondrous wish fulfillment of not one but two diaper pails. This fly crib was souped up with leather armchairs, flat-screen TVs and all the hottest, hippest must-see channels: PBS Kids Sprout, Nick Jr. -- the works, baby!

And that's not all. This platinum parenting paradise took even elite privileges into consideration. Breast-feeding stalls with pumping outlets were fitted with privacy curtains. Double thick, y'all! It sure beats the time I blew the car battery pumping in my Jeep on a lunch break. If one had to be topless, this room was the place to do it.

I should have known my life was heading down this path of parental impropriety. A life in which bathroom talk consumes all my talk. In which a Family Changing Station becomes the Holy Grail to my IndyMama Jones.

The first leg to my utopian discovery kicked off Thursday, when I got a text from a friend I met in birthing class.

"What are you guys doing Saturday? Wanna take the kids to the mall to hang out in the play area?"

It had been a long time since my husband and I had a play date with anyone. Road tripping to a mall a half-hour away and eating in a food court sounded akin to a romantic evening of dancing and downing cocktails. I was all in.

"It's like we are 15," my friend said as we waited in line at the indoor carousel. "What adult texts and asks if you want to hang out at the mall?"

"Adults with kids," I thought. "That's who."

It was during our dinner in the food court that my girlfriend disappeared to find a place to change her son and returned to tell us about Atlantis. A little slice of utopia among mall madness. A family changing room of such unforetold beauty that it may be the true cause behind the Trojan War.

"Dude, you guys have to check it out," she said.

I never have been so eager to change my son's diaper. I picked up my son, refusing to let this opportunity pass me by.

"No, I want to see it," my husband said. He had seen the dark days of trying to change diapers in men's rooms with no changing tables. He needed something to believe in, something to hang his hope on before we got to the age of potty training.

"I want to go, too," said my friend's husband.

"We can all go," said my friend.

And we did.

The six of us reached the room of legend -- three of us afraid of the disappointment that could be waiting there, afraid it would not meet our expectations. But there was no reason to fear. There it stood, the place of miracles. The most beautiful Family Changing Station that ever was.

After absorbing the intricate details of bunny wallpaper and bookshelves, we sat down in the plush chairs. We put our feet up, put our heads back, let out audible sighs of comfort as our babies played with toys on the carpeted floor. And we opened up to one another in the way few parents do. We didn't share the wondrous moments of parenting. Instead, we exchanged horrific diaper changing stories the way veterans talk about war only after they are back in the comfort and safety of home. It was magical. It was relaxing. It was the stuff diaper dreams are made of.

"Next time we come to the mall, we should eat in here," my husband said.

We all nodded. Because we meant it. Because we are parents.

Ode to 1

Mommy, Daddy having fun.
Seeing countries one by one.
What could make our life more grand?
A little gift from babyland.
Mommy paces the store aisle.
Cashier checks out with a smile.
Two minutes is a real long time
When waiting for a blue plus sign.
Now Daddy's biting.
Mommy's scarfing.
So much waiting,
So much barfing.
Why does nine months go so slow?
Mommy can't remember toes.
Finally, the big day came.
Doctor asks, "Is there a name?
It's time to meet your little boy."
Mommy, Daddy filled with joy.
Six pounds and nine ounces strong,
Nineteen and a half inches long.
Fully covered in purple goo
With pink lips and eyes of blue.
Baby sleeps all through the night.
"Am I holding him all right?"
Nurse says, "It's time to go back home
And take care of Baby on your own."
Why is he crying? What can we do?
Does he want food? Did he go No. 2?
Why'd they let us take home this li'l guy?
Shouldn't we have to first get certified?
Mommy, Daddy track the moon.

40

Three a.m. feels like afternoon.
Uh-oh. Baby's bum unleashed its wrath.
Daddy draws yet another bath.
Morning comes, and Baby smiles.
Daddy lets Mommy sleep awhile.
Baby yawns with pinup girl grace.
Who couldn't love that scrunched-up face?
Small victories feel like big wins.
Was that gas, or was that a grin?
Sat up! Rolled over! Held up his own head!
Oh, my gosh, he actually went to bed!
Baby grows at accelerated pace.
Daddy deciphers Baby's likes and tastes.
Bounce on the yoga ball; play the Ramones.
Turn on baseball; hand over the phones.
Little Baby growing up so fast.
His infant days have almost passed.
It's been a year since the day
A "sweet angel" came down to play.
Mommy, Daddy having fun
With their little man, who's turning 1.
Their life couldn't be more grand
Since getting their gift from babyland.

Toddling Toward Toddlerhood

When my son turned 1, friends bought me books on parenting toddlers.

"Turning 1 means the ONEderful days are over," my friend said. "Soon as he toddles, he's a toddler."

I scoffed. How could my precious baby be associated with the sheer terror associated with the nefarious T-word? How could my angel be corralled into a group so vile, so heinous, it makes grown men weep and women cross their legs, swearing they'll have the one child and the one child only. Not my little man. Not him. Not yet. It was too soon. Fingers crossed, toddlerhood was eons away.

The parenting book insisted otherwise, stating that days of archetypal toddlerhood were closer than I thought, asserting that those dreaded evil years were just a few months away. Stephen King

41

could learn a thing or two about writing horror from parenting books.

Looking at my sweet angel, covered in blue icing from his chocolate birthday cake, I questioned the likelihood of his harboring some inner gremlin. He had been chill since the day he was born. His sweet disposition set. His go-with-the-flow character established. Perhaps the onset of toddling brought out the jagged-toothed monster in some children, but not in mine. My son, I decided, was predisposed for awesomeness.

Then the collapsing began.

Seemingly overnight, my son decided that life is awfully dramatic. Too dramatic for rational thought. So dramatic, in fact, that he couldn't take it standing up. Like Scarlett O'Hara, he thought that bad news was best dealt with by faux fainting. He would collapse on the floor, literally at the drop of a hat; one time, we were playing peekaboo by covering my son's eyes with an oversize adult cap, and when the hat dropped from his head and hit the floor, my son hit the floor beside it.

I tried to rationalize it away. This simply meant my child has a sympathetic heart. He didn't want that poor cap to be on the floor all alone. He was simply providing company! This in no way signified pending toddlerdom. After all, toddlers are known for full tantrums -- kicking and screaming on the floor. When my son hit the ground, he always remained silent.

Then the crying began.

The tears didn't accompany the dramatic collapses; they came on their own, fast and frequent. If my son let go of a balloon and it floated to the ceiling, he would be in hysterics. It didn't matter that I handed it back to him within seconds. If he eagerly nodded when I offered him a drink, his excitement would instantly melt to tears in the minute it took me to pour milk into his sippy cup. Oh, the tragedy of it all!

As a mother, I try to empathize with my son's emotions. And sometimes, I really think I get where he's coming from. A balloon floating from your grasp teaches a difficult life lesson in how transitory life is. We are all nomadic balloons, forced to travel through this world alone, without someone to guide our string -- or something like that. And having to wait for your sippy cup is equally tragic because, um, well, because milk is delicious. And it comes from cows. And who doesn't like cows? Am I right?

The months toddled on, but my justifications for my baby's cries and collapses held strong. My son was not becoming a toddler. The proof was in the fact that he had yet to have a tantrum, having never combined tears with the flailing fits. His floor fits remained silent, and his tears came while he stood stoically still.

"Perhaps this will be as bad as it gets," I told myself.

If I'm being completely honest, I secretly hoped my son's behavioral development would be slightly stunted -- at least when it came to tantrums. Nothing too drastic, just by a few years or so. All I'm saying is that if he didn't begin acting like a toddler until he left for college, would it really be so bad? His fraternity brothers could easily excuse his full-blown tantrums on his latest keg-athon, and I would have my sweet angel for the duration of his time at home.

I hoped and prayed. In vain.

As we were leaving the house this morning, my son's sneaker fell off. He hit the ground flailing. And crying. Together.

Have mercy. Toddlerhood has arrived.

The Gift

Michael doesn't know me. He doesn't know my socio-economic status or where I grew up. He doesn't know my marital status or how many kids I have. He doesn't know my triumphs or my failures. Michael doesn't know me. And I don't know Michael. But Michael has changed my life.

A couple of weeks ago, I took my 20-month-old to breakfast at my favorite diner. After the man sitting in the booth across from mine paid for his meal, he walked back toward my table holding a white receipt.

"I paid your bill."

"Thank you," I said, the confusion audible in my voice.

"Do you know why I paid your bill?" he asked.

I shook my head.

"Because you're taking such good care of that little boy."

My eyes welled as he handed me the credit card receipt, proof of his payment, before walking out the door. And there was the stranger's name: Michael.

I had read plenty of stories online about angels disguised as humans stepping up to financially assist someone in need. I've always believed I would be the kind of person who would help if ever presented with the opportunity.

Michael's unexpected gesture made me realize I had been waiting for the "right" moment to be generous when I should have been living generously all along. Clearly, this must be the lesson life was handing me in the form of free French toast. I became determined to pay it forward. ASAP!

My first chance presented itself at Starbucks. I stalked a guy studying drink options for 20 minutes. When he finally shuffled toward the cashier, I jumped in front of him, ordered my drink and offered to pay for whatever he was getting.

The stranger refused, clearly convinced his creepy stalker was trying to poison his drink.

"I insist," I said, unwilling to lose this opportunity to do good. "Someone paid for my breakfast the other day, and I'm just paying it forward."

"No means no!" he yelled.

Perhaps paying for a stranger's coffee wasn't the answer.

I'm not one to make sentimental attachments to inanimate things, but I inexplicably had kept the receipt. Pulling it out of my wallet, my eyes welled again. Why did this silly receipt make me cry? I didn't understand the emotional reaction I was having to my free meal.

That is, until I allowed myself to admit the truth. It wasn't the payment that had touched my heart; it was this stranger's reason for doing so. "Because you're taking such good care of that little boy."

Over breakfast, my son and I had gone through our typical daily routine. He threw crayons on the ground. I picked them up. He threw them again. I took them away. He cried. I made him promise not to throw them. He kept his word. And opted to eat the crayons instead. He wanted to walk around the diner. We did. He wanted to sit on my lap. He did. He slapped my face. I told him to "show Mommy gentle." He petted my cheek and gave me a kiss. We sang songs. And tickled. And giggled. He went in the highchair. And out of the highchair. And in and out again. And that's where my son was -- sitting on my lap, picking at my meal -- when Michael came over. He had seen the whole thing. He had witnessed the cuddles and witnessed the scolding. And after all that, he told me I was doing a good job taking care of my little boy. And it made me cry because it was something I needed to hear -- something probably every parent needs to hear.

After this realization, I began seeing the world differently. I looked for the everyday hero in other people instead of trying to see the hero in myself.

When my son threw a tantrum, I noticed the people who smiled with knowing empathy rather than the nasty glares that I would have only noticed before, whether they had actually been there or not. I looked people in the eye more. Held the door open more. Smiled more. And when a neighbor I'd never met apologized profusely after her toddler ran into my lawn and threw our ball into the street, I told her not to worry, because, I said, "It looks to me like you're doing a good job raising the little boy." And I meant it. And I noticed how her eyes welled when I said it.

I hope to someday thank Michael for the gift he gave me. So much more than a meal, so much more than a compliment, Michael gave me the gift of sight. And if I ever have the opportunity to pay for his meal, I'll try not to be a super-creepy stalker about it.

Baby Cat Crawl

They say, "Do what you love, and love what you do."

I have always been a believer of that concept. It's been my marching order, a goal to work toward. It's a quality I hope to instill in my son.

As a new parent, I've often found myself thinking about my son's future employment, his every newly discovered skill serving as a jumping-off point for my fantasy. When he first rolled over, I thought he might become a gymnast. When he became infatuated with eating twigs, I knew he'd become a conservationist. And when he erased all the apps from my phone, it became unmistakably evident that this little savant was the next Steve Jobs. As his mother, I have made the unwavering commitment to support and encourage any activity he falls in love with and lead him toward a career of doing what he loves with steadfast dedication. A commitment I may regret.

My baby boy wants to be a stripper.

Early Saturday morning, my son and I were watching reruns of a show I used to watch during my childhood. The commercials aired were for weight-loss pills and diet shakes, clearly aimed at moms like me, nostalgic for our own childhoods, sitting on the couch, crying into cereal bowls precariously balancing on the baby-weight bulge we have yet to lose. Or so hope the folks behind these commercials.

Attempting to play into our postpartum psyche, a commercial popped up for pole dancing lessons, an opportunity to get our sexy back. And it was at this point that my 21-month-old son scooted his bottom off the couch, walked over to the TV and stared at the gyrating woman in her underwear.

The stripper slid off her pole and began scantily cat crawling across the floor, and that is how my son came to find his newest obsession: the striptease. Following the stripper's every move, my son got down on all fours, arched his back and flipped his hair back and forth. I was both horrified and disappointed that I didn't have my camera.

The 30-second commercial ended, but my son was hooked. He would toss his hair and laugh. Shake his booty and giggle. Sure, this move wasn't entirely new. My kid would occasionally head-bang on all fours when a particularly rockin' song came on, but now that he had seen stripping as a viable career option, his dance moves seemed tainted. Now every time he took off his clothes and ran around the house, it was as if he were screaming, "Hey, Ma, I found my calling! And I found $1 bills in my diaper!"

My son the stripper. Where had I gone wrong? He was going to be a conservationist, not a cast member in "Thunder From Down Under"! Did I dress him in too many layers during the winter months, giving a subconscious need to rip them all off? In my excitement to give him his toy fire station, had I neglected to assess the irrevocable damage caused by the shiny pole in the center?

I wondered whether I would have to stick to my previous commitment of supporting my son in any life path he chooses. In order to be a good mother, would I have to bedazzle G-strings and hem pants that can be ripped off?

The concept behind doing what you love and loving what you do is rooted in the desire for happiness -- the only thing we parents tout as our desire for our children. But is that real? I don't only want happiness for my child; I want a million things. I want for him education and adventure and love and self-confidence and courage and humor and comfort in his own skin. And if showing off that skin is what makes him happy, I hope I can lead him in the direction of streaking on the football field during the homecoming game instead of streaking for a living and guide him toward following the career path of a different love.

And, my boy, when you are college-bound and choose to relive your first childhood love by mooning the parents at your high-school graduation, I promise to applaud that bare bum, bragging that I made those cheeks. Now that's a commitment I can keep.

F Is for Truck

Driving my son to day care, I was cut off by an oversize pickup truck. I slammed on the brakes and screamed, "Whoa!"

My 21-month-old screamed, "Truck!"

Only he didn't say truck. He said a four-letter word that rhymes with truck.

"What did you just say?" I asked my son.

"Truck!"

Only he didn't say truck.

"Do you mean 'honk'?" I asked, hoping, begging, pleading to the universe that my son had simply twisted a few consonants and vowels. "The cars go honk. Right, baby?"

"No!" my sweet angel yelled back defiantly. "Truck! Truck, truck, truck, truck. TRUCK!"

Only he wasn't saying truck.

Clearly, my son had been in the car enough times when I slammed on the brakes to know that "whoa" wasn't the proper reaction.

I didn't know what to do. Unwilling to reinforce the behavior by reacting to the word, I did the only logical thing I could think of: I belted "The Wheels on the Bus" at the top of my lungs.

My child just stared at me, completely confused.

It's a special moment in a parent's life when your darling babe utters his first curse word. I think of it as one of those stereotypical milestones you hope your kid will never cross, such as trying his first cigarette or getting pregnant on her prom night.

Not to say I didn't know this day would come eventually. I had just hoped he would have at least turned 2. And I'd hoped, perhaps foolishly, that his first curse word would be "ship" or "crab" or "dam." Only not really ship or crab or dam. I had hoped his first offense would be a little less offensive. But not my child. He went straight for the gold.

My friends kindly invoked their finest acting chops and asked snark-free, "Where did he learn that word?" But they knew the answer. My son had learned it from listening to me.

I work in an industry of words, and for some ironic reason, we people who have the entire dictionary at our disposal are most loyal to the sinful seven. It is embraced in my world. Accepted. Rewarded, even.

For months now, my husband and I have been saying we need to start being mindful of our potty mouths. We knew, at some point, our beautiful boy would want to copy the fun words Mommy and Daddy say when they are speaking most animatedly. We told ourselves to watch what we say, but we didn't watch what we said. And now here I was, screaming "The Wheels on the Bus" at my foulmouthed baby.

There have been very few times in my life when I have felt truly ashamed of my chosen vocabulary. There was a time or two when I threw my hand over my mouth, mortified, after cursing in front of a child old enough to understand what I was saying. And the time at the Vatican when I was so moved by seeing Pope John Paul II that I exclaimed, "That was trucking awesome!" Which wouldn't have been so horrible if I had actually said the word truck -- which I hadn't -- or if the exclamation hadn't been caught by a local news crew, which it had.

However, I have never been more ashamed than I was when I walked up to my son's Lutheran day care, took the teachers aside, including the pastor's wife, and told them my son drops F-bombs.

In the split second between my confession and my waiting for their reaction, I thought of an article I had read about a preschooler expelled for cursing because of the school's zero-tolerance policy. Would my son's day care react similarly? Could this go on his permanent record? What if no other day care facilities would admit my potty-mouthed mini-me? I'd have to quit my job and stay home with him. My lack of teaching skills would be exposed. He would be the only kid starting kindergarten who couldn't count to 10 or recognize colors. His entire education would be a stressful game of catch-up, ending in his dropping out of high school to start a rap career. His debut album would be titled "F Is for Truck." Literally, truck. But it wouldn't be an ironic title; my son would actually mean the word "truck" because he never learned to spell.

Luckily, the teachers simply laughed. "Don't worry. Just try to be more careful at home."

I promised. Abso-trucking-lutely.

The Black Widow

Parents who laugh at their crying kids are jerkfaces.

Lists about "stupid things kids cry about," including pictures of toddlers wailing over something the parents deemed ridiculous, are always trending on the Web. And I hate them. Those parents should have their reproducing rights revoked.

How could any good parent whip out a camera rather than offer a hug? Sure, the kid is a slobbering, sobbing mess simply because he's not being allowed to wear his mother's maxi pads as stickers. But so what? It's not funny to the child, so it's not funny to me.

At least, that's how I used to feel.

Dear Laughing Parents: So sorry about that whole revoking your procreating permit line. And really, hate is a strong word. You see, I was looking down on you from the luxury of not yet having a full-on toddler. My son just turned 2, and tantrums are new to me. Please forgive my ignorance. I now understand that sometimes there is hilarity in the hysteria.

A few days ago, I was doing some gardening and came across a black widow and her egg sac by the windowsill outside my home. I did what any rational adult would do: I screamed, jumped back about 10 feet and wondered whether it was time to change my decision about gun ownership. While my whole body shook as if trying to shake off the spider that I could still visibly see in her web, I considered whether torching the entire lawn would be too drastic of a move. I certainly wouldn't want the house to catch fire, but I thought it might be worth the risk.

While I was contemplating whether to call the fire department before or after I set fire to the yard, my son took a few strides toward the spider, arms outstretched, as if he were Shaggy running away from some scary, ghostly, monstrous beasts. *And I would've gotten away with it, too, if it weren't for you meddling kids and that dog, Scooby Doo.* Only in this case, the monstrous beast was real, and "getting away with it" meant the hatching of her millions of baby black widows, who would come to infest our home and take us hostage in their webs, baiting us so many times that our bodies would turn into a living Twister mat for their eight-legged amusement.

What? I have it on good authority that kid spiders play Twister, too.

My son's advances toward the spider pulled me out of my nightmarish reverie. Before he grabbed the black widow, I pulled him back. He looked at me with hurt curiosity. Why wouldn't I let him hold the pretty spider with the red hourglass design aggressively protecting her egg sac? She seemed like a great new friend.

I crouched down and told my son that there are two different kinds of spiders -- good spiders (I lied) and bad spiders. Bad spiders can hurt you, and this was a bad spider. And then, just to drive home the point, I said the magic words: "No touch."

To which my not-so-terrible but very 2-year-old son said with indignant determination, "Yes, touch."

A giggle escaped.

I couldn't help it. He was so cute in his suicidal ambition. Smiling, I said, "No. No touch. That spider can hurt you."

"Touch the spider," he wailed, lunging for the web again.

I held him back, at which point my son dropped to the ground, thrashing, sobbing, choking on the words, "Touch bwack winnow spider."

And I laughed.

My husband came around the corner with a garbage bag to take away the spider after we cut the branch holding the web and egg sac off the bush. Burning down the house became our plan B. As my husband came into sight, I called out, "Do you have your phone on you? We have to get a picture of this kid!"

My son and I were both hysterical, just in very different ways. I didn't get down on my knees to hug my sobbing child. I mean, I did. Just not right away. Not before the potential of a photo op was addressed -- which, sadly, was not captured.

But I'm not too concerned; we'll get a crazy-kid-crying picture eventually -- especially because my son is on an obsessive hunt for a bwack winnow spider to cuddle.

Excuse me while I have a heart attack.

A Late-Night Mommy Call

There are only two groups of people who make plans to go out after 10 p.m.: those answering a booty call and moms. It's possible there is a third group composed of moms looking for a booty call, but based on my expertise from being a parent for 2 1/2 years, I'm going to say that is very unlikely.

And I know what you are thinking: "What about the vampires?" To this, I say A) they are not people, and B) I'm pretty sure they fall into one of the two groups. I've seen "True Blood." Those sexy Nordic blood hounds are only after one thing, and it doesn't include calling you in the morning or meeting your mother.

Prior to marrying my husband and having my son, I was familiar with late-night meetup plans. Back when the streetlamps lit up an evening of possibility. I creatively coined that time "college."

Little did I know back then that sharing the moonlit roads with me were moms. Moms! Moms who were possibly less dressed than I was. Not intentionally, of course. They had just simply forgotten to put on pants that day.

Moms, as I have now discovered, take to the streets at these scandalous hours because -- wait for it -- it's the only time they can.

By the time I'm done working my full-time job, spending time with my kid, making dinner, reading books with him, bathing him, going through his bedtime routine and cleaning up the daily damage of my toddler tornado, it's a miracle if I can leave the house by 9:30 p.m. So 10 p.m. is what I aim for. That's when I plead for my friends to meet me.

"My mom told me only bad things happen when someone asks to see you after prime-time TV has ended," my friend said in her typical dry, sarcastic Daria tone.

"We don't have to go out," I said. "You can come over here, or I can go to your house."

"Mrs. Langrock, are you trying to seduce me?"

Oh, if only.

My late-night hangout sessions are a product of necessity and wonderfully pathetic. There is no heavy partying or drinking as one might infer by the late hour. The visits are short, as I have either work in the morning or a toddler who simply needs to build a pirate ship with blocks before the sun comes up. There is no dressing up, dressing down or undressing. There is no loud music or dancing; on the rare occasions I get to see my friends, I'm not apt to waste them by not being able to hear a word they say. There is no spontaneity. No seeing where the night takes us. It is a very calculated plan to not disappear from my social life in two-hour increments across many months of late-night rendezvous.

There is a reason I didn't notice the late-night moms when I was younger. It's that there is really nothing to notice. The moms may be headed to an exciting evening of Boggle and Apples to Apples, but the non-mom's evening promises to involve far more games.

And though these booty call receptionists don't see me walking the city streets, I love seeing them -- especially when the girls trip on their stilettos. But even when I'm being partially blinded by the full moonlight reflecting off their copious bling, I enjoy the sight.

There is a joy in watching the younger, the untethered -- a joy that comes from feeling that in this moment, I know I've done something right. Passing the non-moms in the streets brings back fond memories. Passing these non-moms on the streets makes me feel alive for being out myself.

Does my body scream at me for sleep deprivation? Yes. Is it effort to leave my house once I've put on slippers and unzipped my pants? Duh.

But on these rare nights, I've decided not to fade into the darkness of mommydom. On these rare nights, I've stayed out late enough to be illuminated by streetlamps. On these rare nights, I'm out on a mommy call.

In the words of the great philosopher Bill Pullman: "We will not go quietly into the night! We will not vanish without a fight! We're going to live on! We're going to survive!"

Granted, he was talking about aliens attacking Earth on Independence Day, not mothers, but I'm pretty sure it still applies.

Owning a Dog Versus Parenting

Since I've become a parent, one thing has been made abundantly clear: Having a baby is not the same as having a dog.

The two cannot compare, no matter how much organic food you blend and spoon-feed your dog, no matter how often your baby chews your favorite shoe and urinates on the kitchen floor.

You may be thinking, "No Shih Tzu, Sherlock." But try telling that to some dog owners.

I have no grievance against people who simply call their pets their babies. It is cute and colloquial and speaks to their affection. I often tell my toddler to be careful around his big brother when he is about to step on Pig, our 18-pound rabbit. And I'm not out to get the people who dress up their dogs like people, teach them to bark greetings and take them to see therapists, masseurs and mediums. I'm silently judging them, naturally, but I hold no ill will.

No, I'm against the adamant aggressors -- the ones who pontificate without provocation about the perfect parallels between parenting a puppy and parenting a baby and claim that if you dare to disagree, you are clearly an enemy of the canine.

Let me be very clear: Babies and doggies are different. We'll start with the slobbery one.

Wait.

Actually, allow me to clarify further: Let's start with the one who walks on all fours.

Nope.

Shoot, that doesn't work, either. I promise you that having a baby is nothing like having a dog! Allow me to try one more time.

Let's start with the furry one:

First of all, a dog has a tail. Second of all, you can leave the dog outside all day while you go to work, to the gym and grocery shopping, and no one is waiting to handcuff you for endangerment upon your return. The baby, on the other hand, is a human being.

Prior to having a baby, I was perturbed by certain dog owners' assertions that owning a pet is the same as parenting. Since becoming a parent, however, I've seen my irritation grow to full-on feverish hatred. Sure, you can love your dog. You can love your dog more than anything in the world. My first dog was, without a doubt, my best friend. He died nearly 15 years ago, and I miss him still. I always will. I'm not interested in combating love. I'm interested in combating their comparing their circumstances to the weight of worry and responsibility and the seismic shift that occurs to your lifestyle, how people perceive you and how you perceive yourself after spawning.

Good friends of mine had their baby about the same time I had my son. Like many couples, they bought a dog as a practice baby, something to lay the groundwork of responsibility and life shifting. There is a reason these pets are called practice.

A couple of months after having her child, my friend exclaimed to me: "Being a parent is so difficult! I thought it would be just like having our dog!"

It was at that time when I reminded her that they sadly had returned their dog a month after adopting it. "I know," she said. "And this is even harder!"

Yes, this is harder. It's much harder. But it gets easier.

Now that my son is 2, it's getting much easier. The most noticeable difference is how he can help out by bringing me things. It's not uncommon that I will ask him to go fetch my slippers or bring me the morning newspaper.

Uh-oh.

OK, let's not get too excited here. Sure, my son will fetch things when I ask, but that's not to say having a child is anything like having a dog. It's not as if my son goes into the garden and digs holes to hide his bones or anything. Rather, my son's favorite activity is playing ball.

Shoot!

OK, yes, dogs like to play ball like my son, but the comparisons really stop there. Dogs go to the bathroom outside, bark to get attention and are crated at night. Whereas my son goes to the bathroom in a diaper, screams to get attention and sleeps in a crib. Take that!

Um, I think I'm starting to see what you're saying, dog owners.

OK, OK, having a baby may be a bit like having a dog. But you cat people are on your own!

Skipping K-12

My co-worker scurried toward her desk, eyes red and puffy. I walked over and asked her what was wrong.

"I'm sure he will be fine," she said, her voice cracking. "It's just. My son. He..." She began sobbing uncontrollably. I looked on, concerned, afraid to ask the follow-up question: What was wrong with her son? Was he hurt? Was he diagnosed with some horrific disease? Did his dad win full custody and take a job in New Zealand? What had happened to cause my co-worker's agonizing pain?

"My baby, he, he..." She gulped down her tears. "He started kindergarten."

I laughed and rolled back on my heels in relief, but I was alone in this sentiment. Other moms who had heard our crying co-worker came running over to offer comfort and share stories of their first-day traumas.

As I watched wrinkles of pain find their old, familiar places on the foreheads of my co-workers while they recounted tales of their now adult children's first day of school, one thing became perfectly clear: I'm not doing it!

Nope. No way. No how. My kid is not going to kindergarten. He's not going school the following year, either. My heart can't take it.

Not that I'd withhold my son's education just for my own emotional stability. Pulling him from school will be for his benefit, of course. If the moms are crying messes dropping off their kids at kindergarten, just imagine the waterfall of woe their tykes must be. Is learning the three R's really worth the turmoil?

I mean, who needs school anyway? When did it become so important? Bill Gates and Steve Jobs were school dropouts, and they became two of the most influential billionaires in the world. If my son never steps foot in a classroom, just imagine how brilliant he will be!

Unfortunately, I can't afford to quit my job and home-school my child, so he will have to come to work with me. But that's fine. I just know he will find Excel sheets as riveting as I do. And what better way to learn to count than by clicking the end of a pen for eight hours a day? Doesn't that sound like fun? If he counts one click for every second of the workday, he will count all the way up to 28,800! Is my kid a genius or what? He can learn his letters using the label-maker every day to mark my food in the company fridge.

As an added educational bonus, the signs outside every door in my building have Braille. Find me a public school teaching *that* to kids. When teachers encourage study-abroad immersion programs to learn another language, I'm pretty sure this is exactly what they have in mind.

Now, there may be some setbacks to my son's education-free existence, but I feel the 24-hour access to his mama more than makes up for it. He may never experience a cafeteria-wide food fight, but my office has vending machines with microwaveable burritos that are changed out monthly. So really, who has the better deal? And though my company doesn't have recess with playgrounds and sandboxes, we do have nice wooden benches with conveniently placed ashtrays to play in. And though it's true that by skipping school my son may never learn to read, I'm confident that with his company-funded cellphone, Siri will ensure he never has to.

Obviously, I'm onto something here. If I weren't, then why would we have Take Our Daughters and Sons to Work Day? And the government supports my initiative to ditch the classroom for the office. Here's proof: President Obama not only works in the White House but also makes his kids *live* in the White House! Talk about helicopter parenting. That guy has issues.

I was about to email human resources regarding our policy on bringing children to work, when my crying co-worker said, "I guess it's just hard for parents. Not the kids. My son was thrilled to be there. It's a milestone we parents have to go through."

I broke through the crowd of reminiscing mothers to ask, "Your kid was happy to be at kindergarten? He wasn't scared? Or crying?"

"No," she said. "Only the parents had tears."

If our kids want an education, I guess we have to give it to them. Good luck out there, parents. Stay strong.

Rock 'n' Roll Mama

Before I became a mommy, I had the same judgmental view of the procreating members of our society that many childless people have: I thought of them as old. Passç. Yesterday's news. Uncool. Not with it. Lame.

I didn't see this as a nerdiness that grows over time, determined by how high the elastic on your mom jeans rides up past your bellybutton. No, I saw moms as dumpy from the moment they are wheeled out of the hospital, bundled baby in arms.

Now that I'm a new mommy, I'm floored as to why our society would push this image of the loser mama, because not to brag, but I have never been more of a rock star.

No, seriously.

When I was in college, a night of partying would inevitably lead to sleeping on my desk during my 8 a.m. class the next day. Drool on my hands, clumped mascara making linebacker lines under my eyes, I'd lament the utter outrageousness of asking students to function so early. It's, like, not even right to torture your students. Ya know?

But now that I'm a parent, I look back on those long nights of partying in college as mere child's play. I used to think one Thursday-night keg stand session warranted a full Friday in bed. Pfft, amateur.

Nowadays, I am up all night, every night, hand wrapped around the bottle. And I don't just stay up late these days. Oh, no, I've got far more rock star status than that. Instead of simply staying up late as I did in my younger years, now I also get up multiple times a night, pulling myself from my warm bed, all in the name of rock(ing my baby to sleep).

If the outrageous sleeping habits of new moms aren't enough to secure every new mom's star on the Hollywood Walk of Fame, the postpartum wardrobe should do it. Designed to elicit jealousy in the most enamored of rock groupies, new mommy clothes are made to be taken off as quickly as possible. Shirts open in the front; bra cups unclip; and pants are buttonless. Everything we wear is made with the intention of easy access. Perfect for Mardi Gras, spring break, breast-feeding your baby and getting your chest signed by your favorite musician.

And I thought going to class in pajamas was sexy.

It doesn't end there. Like a rock star on tour, I have mastered the 60-second shower, sing the same few songs every night and often wear the same clothes a few days in a row -- occasionally inside out and backward. Because, ya know, like a rock star, I get dressed in the dark.

Rock stars have women throw their bras at them onstage. Sleep-deprived, I occasionally forget to wear a bra. They trash hotel rooms; my bedroom is constantly trashed by an onslaught of Cheerios and

Goldfish. They are often found with drugs on them. I, too, travel with zip-close bags filled with white powder. The lifestyle similarities are endless.

Perhaps it is not the similarities between new moms and rock stars that should be surprising but rather their differences. We moms live this totally crazy rock-style life without groupies, roadies or any other kind of assistance. While the younger, cooler, childless demographic chugs energy drinks and pops Adderall to keep up with all the tasks at hand, new moms run on adrenaline. Rocking our jobs, bills, baby care, projects, chores, mealtime, cleanup, playtime, discipline, hugs, baths and shopping while relying solely on the pulsating energy generated from knowing that if you slack, if you drop the ball, you will bring on the apocalypse. Now, how rock 'n' roll is that?

It's time we change the world's perception of the mommy and have everyone see us as we truly are. Masters of our own REM cycle. Energy-infused. Bottle-clutching. White powder-toting. Occasionally braless. Multitasking wonder women.

Yes, as the years drag on, we may lose our cool a bit. We may wear jeans with elastic bands and use the wrong slang words. We may have outdated hairstyles and struggle to keep up on the latest tween star. We may not always catch all the balls we have in the air. But that doesn't mean we aren't just like rock stars.

Case in point:

Mick Jagger totally wears mom jeans.

~ ~ ~

Chapter 4

"On Wednesdays, We Wear Jeans": Attire

PajamaJeans Obsession

The first time I saw an ad for PajamaJeans, I was vegging out on the couch with one of my best friends. When the commercial ended, she looked at me incredulously and said, "That was a joke, right?"

I placed my hand over my heart and said, "I certainly hope not!"

Never before had I seen a product designed with specifically me in mind. It was as if someone had hired a private investigator to leaf through my diaries and rifle through my closets. Then that PI married a psychotherapist, who unraveled the innermost workings of my subconscious desires, fears and motivations. And when the private investigator and psychotherapist made sweet love, they gave birth to my beloved PajamaJeans.

The PajamaJeans were my new must-have. I thought about them constantly. Thought about the adventures we would go on -- trips to the park, maybe a game of basketball followed by some much-deserved sprawling out on the couch or snuggling under the covers. I thought about taking them for a ride on my imaginary motorcycle, taking them camping, sleeping under the stars and then having a nice tumble at the laundromat. These weren't just pajamas. They weren't just jeans. They were PajamaJeans, damn it. Soul mate pants, if you ask me.

Sure, I'd had PajamaJeans-esque experiences in my past. There was a time when I wore pajama bottoms out of the house nearly every day. Those years were called high school. And yeah, I also went through a phase in which I passed out regularly in my jeans. Those years were called college. But in neither of those instances did I have permission to be so unabashedly lazy and slovenly and simultaneously socially acceptable. PajamaJeans had a national commercial, for goodness' sake! Twelve million buyers can't be wrong! OK, I have no idea how many people have bought PajamaJeans, but it must be enough to keep those commercials on my television nightly, taunting me, seducing me.

So when my guy surprised me with a baby-blue package, I was over the moon. It was more beautiful than a Tiffany-blue box. It was

PajamaJeans-blue! Inside were a pair of medium PajamaJeans and a complimentary T-shirt.

I ran to try them on, ready to wear them for the day. Ready to wear them for life! I could have cried; I was brimming with so much excitement.

As one can assume, given such joyful anticipation, the pain that welled up in my heart and at the back of my throat when the pants of my dreams did not fit is too hard to put into words.

I always have been tall and slender. I'm not a giant, but my body basically goes head, shoulders, legs, feet. I skip the torso altogether. My junior-high years were spent in high-water pants, long before they were popular. And the PajamaJeans brought back a flood of painful childhood memories. The PajamaJeans that had stolen my heart could barely cover my butt, snagged at the crotch and ending mid-shin. I could almost hear the kids calling out, "Katiedid Long Legs. Spider Girl."

My dreams of a mutual tumble at the laundromat came to an abrupt and devastating halt. I never would get to wear the PajamaJeans shopping or become that mom-on-the-go as the commercial advertised. Now I know how people who finish in fourth place at the Olympics feel: You come so close to the dream you can taste it, and then cruelly, unfairly, it is taken from you.

I sent my would-be soul mate pants back to their manufacturer. I thought about trying a bigger size, but my fear of a second round of disappointment was too great.

Maybe I will use the money I was refunded to buy a Forever Lazy. The folks in those commercials always look pretty happy, tailgating before the game or reading a book by the fire. A sleeved blanket that zips couldn't possibly let me down like the PajamaJeans, could it? Then again, maybe I need to give my heart a moment to heal before looking for a replacement to my first love.

Everything in its time. Everything in its time.

Freedom Pants

My life is changed forever! I just made the most amazing, groundbreaking, life-altering, dream-granting discovery:

Pregnancy pants.

Perhaps some of you remember my previous column in which I declared my undying love for PajamaJeans. Oh, silly youth. How

I've matured since then.

For those of you who don't know, pregnancy pants look like normal pants from the hips down. But rather than have a zipper or buttons that come up near the waist -- securing the pants on your body -- they have a massive elastic band that reaches halfway up your ribcage. This band of glory holds up your pants and enables you to get fat, fatter and then fattererer without ever having to buy new pants! Amazing, right?

The only issue I have with my new beloved is their marketing. Whoever is responsible for getting the word out about pregnancy pants (and pregnancy jeans, pregnancy skirts, pregnancy shorts, etc.) is doing an abysmal job.

First of all, pregnancy pants should not be restricted to women's wear only. Are you seriously implying that men could not use a little freedom in the gut region? Buttons and zippers are so overrated.

I say we open up the market to both men and women. Here are some other demographics I think pregnancy pants should be marketed to:

--Newlyweds. So, you dropped 30 pounds for the wedding. Congratulations. She looked beautiful in her dress; he looked dashing in his tux; you went on your honeymoon and took a million pictures in your equally skimpy bathing suits, which you will someday shove in the faces of your children to show them how skinny you were before parenthood ruined your metabolism. But let's get real here for a second, shall we? It wasn't just the births of children that left the skimpy swimwear buried at the bottom of your sock drawer. In the first year of marriage, you gained back the 30 pounds you lost for the wedding. Naturally! By the second year of marriage, you've added on another 20 pounds. Good for you! You're happy. And really, whom are you trying to impress anymore? The only bummer is that with 50 pounds of extra weight, the clothing bills have started adding up. But they wouldn't have if you had bought pregnancy pants before the big day. With pregnancy pants, husband and wife can gain their 50-plus without ever hitting the mall. Now that's a lifetime vow I can get behind.

--College students. Freshman 15 got ya down? Who wants to spend money at the mall as a broke college student? Being able to afford nothing but ramen noodles and beer is what got you into this mess in the first place! Buy your recent high-school graduate a couple of pairs of pregnancy pants. Then, whether she gains the freshman 15 or the freshman 15 every semester of college, she won't need to waste her food money on jeans.

--Frat boys. If your son is about to join a fraternity, do him a favor and buy him an extra pair of pregnancy pants. Something will have to hold in that growing beer gut.

--Kleptomaniacs. Don't you just hate when you're trying to steal something from a store and the item just keeps sliding out of the bottom of your shirt? Never again when you have your elastic partner in crime, pregnancy pants. They will hold your stolen goods close to your abdomen, with no chance for slippage. Don't spend another night in jail with pregnancy pants.

And it doesn't stop there! If you are a buffet lover, were recently divorced, recently retired, were just kicked off the Olympic speed skating team, have a desk job, are a competitive speed-eater, are a yo-yo dieter or are a puffer fish, pregnancy pants are for you! And could we please market these for the holiday season? What would be more comfortable than wearing a comfy pair of pregnancy pants before sitting down to a big Thanksgiving dinner? It's what the Native Americans would've wanted.

In my last effort to ditch the stigma associated with pregnancy pants, I'd like to abandon their gender-specific name and call them freedom pants. I can't think of anything more American than strapping on a pair of freedom pants and helping yourself to a fourth serving. Let freedom pants ring.

Beauty Is Pain

Many moons ago, I made a promise to myself that I would not pass on my insecurities, my complexes or my dose of crazy to my child. I declared that I would never stand before a mirror, with my child by my feet, and insult my looks or my intelligence or my worth. I promised myself that even on my weakest days, I would keep up an appearance of strength, confidence and grace.

Oops.

A year and a half into this whole parenting thing and I have broken my promise, passing on my deepest, darkest complex, born from years of humiliation and harassment, to my son: fear of short pants.

I won't put my son in pants that show ankle! You can't make me do it!

I was always the tall kid. During my adolescence, long-sized pants did not exist. And if they did, they still were not long enough for my lanky limbs. I spent my childhood being told how lucky I was to be "all leg." But when I was 13, grunge was in, and capri pants were the opposite of cool. The only advice my mom gave to cope with the fact that every pair of pants I owned ended mid-shin was to pull up my socks. So I did. I pulled up my socks as high as they would go. Often, my socks ended before my pants began. If you are not a visual person and are having a hard time imagining this, allow me to fill in the gaps: I looked ridiculous -- every day. It didn't help that I rarely could find matching socks.

Kids called me Katiedid Longlegs -- and then it was Daddy Longlegs. Which led to Spider-woman and ended at Black Widow Spider. Better watch out! Black Widow is coming!

I would try everything I could to cover my ankles. I let out the hem on the bottom of my pants; that got me an inch. I sewed additional fabric onto the bottom of my jeans, giving it a bell-bottom look. Not very trendy in the grunge-centric '90s. Eventually, I realized I lived with a choice: I could cover my ankles or cover my bum. I chose to cover my ankles. I bought pants in sizes too big so I could pull them down low enough to cover my ankles. I then wore long shirts to cover my derriere. Most of the time, this worked. But on a few occasions, my shirt would get hiked up, and my bare bottom would be fully exposed for all of junior high to see. Black Widow Spider would become Butt Widow Spider.

I cursed my mother, blaming her genetics. I swore I would never, ever tell my insufficiently attired child to simply pull up his socks.

By the time high school started, long jeans became accessible. Even the longs were not quite long enough, but they sufficed. Capris came into fashion, but the mere thought of putting them on gives me an anxiety attack to this day. I've been too traumatized to go down the short-panted path again.

Which brings me to my son. At 18 months old, he's too short for his 24-month pants, but (conundrum alert!) his ankles show in the 18-month pants. Every morning, we spend at least 20 minutes while I get him dressed, do the ankle check, determine the pants are too short and try again until I finally settle on one of the too-big 24-month pairs. Sure, the bottom cuffs I make inevitably come undone –- not to mention he is too skinny around the waist to hold up his slacks -- but aren't a few daily stumbles on the playground worth having covered ankles?

My husband doesn't seem to think so. He is advocating keeping him in the "better-fitting" 18-month jeans for the simple and insignificant reason that our child doesn't fall when in them.

Last week, I reiterated my concern that my son will be referred to as a poisonous arachnid. My husband replied: "No one will call him that. When his socks are pulled up, you can't even see his ankles."

We are no longer on speaking terms.

I may not be able to keep my promise of not passing down all of my insecurities, complexes and idiosyncratic fear of exposed ankles to my child. But I will hold true to my 13-year-old self. No one will ever tell my baby to pull up his socks.

Beauty is pain.

A Big Fashion Choice

I am an addict.

They say the first step is admitting that you have a problem. I do, and it's time to come clean. I love wearing maternity clothes.

In case you are wondering, I'm not pregnant again. But you wouldn't know it by my wardrobe. By my wardrobe, you could mistake me for Michelle Duggar from "19 Kids and Counting."

You may not think that maternity shopaholism is that sexy of a disease; it doesn't have the immediate universal flair of chocaholism. But you couldn't be more wrong.

There's something sensual about the tug of the forgiving spandex-blend material when I pull on the waist of a hanging garment to check the tag. A heat rush burns my cheeks as my eyes settle on the tag's large "M" for "maternity." A tickle of naughtiness creeps up my spine when I curl the pull string of a maternity shirt around my little finger. Tugging it. Releasing the bow, liberating the shirt -- the released fabric cascading to newfound freedom in every direction. I simply can't describe the feeling of wholeness and centeredness I get from wearing clothes that seemingly float around me. It's like wearing a puffy cloud of love.

Do I daydream about emptying dressers full of expandable pants and belly belts onto my bed and rolling around in their elastic goodness? Of course. Who doesn't? But my addiction runs much deeper than the simple joy of wearing oversize garments. I love the rush I get from ignoring my Target shopping list and walking straight into the maternity aisle, hands immediately wrapping around a purple turtleneck with an expandable neck. It's naughty. It's wrong. I don't belong in this section of the store. But before I know it, I have a cartful of clothes and I'm full-speed booking it to the checkout line.

Don't judge. I finally have found my style, my image, my look. If only I had discovered the simple joy of shopping for maternity clothes early in my teen years! I could have avoided the pain of walking around in whatever tacky trends my mom bought for me. (OK, sure, I might have bemoaned the reason behind my pubescent discovery of stretchy pants, but clothes would have been a definite silver lining.) All of those years my friends threatened to send in my pictures to TLC's "What Not to Wear" would have disappeared! Stacy London always says that once you know how it feels to be in perfectly fitted jeans, you never will go back. And now I know, Stacy! Really, I know! And it comes equipped with a 5-inch stretchy bellyband and four rows of buttons to accommodate a growing gut. I realize that London probably wouldn't recommend wearing maternity jeans a year after giving birth, but she probably never has put on a pair, so what does that hussy know?

For the first 30 years of my life, I hated shopping. Loathed it. Despised it. And now I am supposed to just give up my new shopping passion just because I'm no longer with child? You know what this is? This is discrimination! I will sue you if you try to stop me! I have rights!

Sorry. Didn't mean to yell. I get a little impassioned over my maternity wear shopaholism. Whew.

I've made a lot of excuses for my addiction over the past year. I told myself it's OK because I haven't lost all the baby weight. The clothes are convenient for a mom who is on the go. Everyone else is doing it. I even have been proud of wearing the tent-sized garments. I'm a revolutionary! An artist! People who think outside the box are always persecuted. Just think about the scandal when women first started wearing pants.

But yesterday, in the Target checkout line, a woman looked at my cartful of maternity clothes and asked, "When is your baby due?"

My cheeks burned red, not from the sexy rush of rolling in muumuus but from that painful and ever-so-distinctive flush of embarrassment. I looked at the woman, smiled and said, "March 19."

Without thinking, I had given her my birthday and scuttled away, quickly returning the clothes to their racks.

They say the first step is admitting you have a problem.

Hello. My name is Katiedid Langrock, and I'm a maternity wear shopaholic.

Jeans and the Death of Trail Etiquette

"What else do you need me to fit in your backpack?"

Yesterday I helped my friend Catherine pack for a hiking trip across the Overland Track in Tasmania, Australia. She came over with her car full of knickknacks, unsure of what to bring and what to leave behind. Fire starters, sleeping bag liners, headlamps, a shovel for bathroom breaks and lacy panties just in case romance strikes in the wilderness.

I created piles: the must-brings, the if-we-can-fit-its and the leave-behinds. Catherine looked at me with concern, peering at her 65-liter backpack.

"The must-haves will fit," I said. "Don't worry."

I spent two years living out of a backpack, including a stint working as an adventure tour guide in Australia. Packing for adventures is my superpower. Mary Poppins' magical purse has nothin' on me.

Years of daily packing and repacking has given me a certain level of expertise when it comes to the important stuff.

"The flask is fine," I told Catherine, "but I'd take a bladder of wine instead. It conforms to the space in your backpack, and after polishing off the bag, you can blow it up to use as a pillow." See? The important stuff.

"Is there room for my jeans?"

"Jeans?!" I scoffed. "There will be no jeans."

My skills have come a long way since the time I packed nearly four months' worth of underwear because I was afraid I wouldn't find a laundromat. Having realized the error of my ways, I unloaded the undergarments with a male friend of mine who was heading home from Europe just as I was arriving. As luck would have it, my friend was stopped at customs and forced to explain why he had a surplus of panties in his luggage. Nearly a decade later, I still smile every time I think about him being pulled aside, his ears turning red from embarrassment.

There are very few things I like to think of myself as an expert on, but my backpack packing is one of them. Which is why I almost choked when Catherine dared to say, "Jeans Guy would've made room for my jeans."

Oh, Jeans Guy, my hiking nemesis.

Backpack packing aficionado or not, most hikers will agree there is a certain code of conduct on the trails. Trail culture dictates you give room for people to embrace their surroundings. You allow people to go at their own pace. And you reserve judgment on nearly everything, from physical appearance to attire, even if they're hiking in something as ridiculous as, say, jeans. Everyone I had ever met on a trail followed trail culture. That is, until I met Jeans Guy.

Jeans Guy and I crossed paths for four days while hiking the Inca Trail to Machu Picchu in Peru. And in that time, he broke nearly every rule of trail etiquette. His stupid head bobbed to the music booming out of his stupid iPod. He would barge past me, allowing me half a second to decide whether I was going to step toward the mountain or the cliff before he made the decision for me. Most annoyingly, Jeans Guy didn't let me enjoy a sense of accomplishment or appreciation for where I was. When I stopped at a beautiful lookout, Jeans Guy came up and said, "This isn't nearly as beautiful as it is on Mount Fuji." When I stopped to catch my breath, he ran past, saying, "I didn't stop when I hiked Mount Kilimanjaro, and that was 10 times harder than this." And when I'd commented on how amazing the Incan ruins were, he said, "Meh. The Mayan ruins are far more impressive." I hated him.

Worst of all, Jeans Guy was a bad influence on me. Now I, too, break one of the rules of trail etiquette. I now judge attire. Whenever I see a person hiking in jeans, I'm reminded of my nemesis and instantly filled with rage. I want to rip the jeans off the person and scream, "These don't wick or dry quickly or zip off to become shorts! You'd be better off hiking in the nude. Or is that not how they do things on Mount Friggin' Fuji?"

"Either the jeans stay or I go," I said to Catherine, dramatically throwing her jeans onto the leave-behind pile.

I said I am an expert on packing. I never said anything about being an expert on maturity.

~ ~ ~

67

Chapter 5

Geek Out With Your Jeep Out: Obsessions

Todd -- A Love Story

Todd is my best friend. Todd is my true love. Todd is my soul mate. Todd is my car.

A khaki-colored, soft-top, stick-shift, no-frills 2003 Jeep Wrangler, to be exact. And I love him.

As a child, I was so obsessed with the Wrangler that my parents would buy me a new Micro Machine version of the car every year for my birthday. My Barbies would sit on top of the tiny metal boxes, waving to Ken, their hair blowing in the wind.

I didn't think I ever would get my Jeep Wrangler. It felt like an unattainable pipe dream, like becoming an astronaut or getting bitten by a ware-kangaroo and changing form every full moon. But as fate would have it, the stars aligned, and Todd and I came together.

Wanting to share the joy of Todd with the rest of the world, I painted his name across his spare tire cover with gold spray paint. World, meet Todd.

And meet him they did.

The amazing thing about my beloved is that he did not just bring infinite joy into my life; he has brought joy into strangers' lives, as well. People are inexplicably drawn to Todd. I've seen folks taking photos of him, full families posing with Todd for a photo. Fellow drivers call out Todd's name as they pass by. I've had celebrities smile and wave at me in Todd, and though I'd love to think the reason is they read my column and recognize my face, I know the truth. Todd is a sexy beast. He has been left more love letters than Justin Bieber.

One time, I was walking back to Todd after finishing the late shift at a bar I was tending, only to find two drunken girls -- who were dressed as if they were looking for more than just a party -- leaning over Todd and giggling. When they spotted me coming toward them, they stumbled away as quickly as their little wasted wobbly legs could take them. Left on Todd was a note that read, "Dear Todd, We think you are crazy sexy. Call us for a good time.

Threesome?" Yes, they left a phone number. No, I did not call it. But I kept the note in Todd's glove compartment. Who am I to throw away something that belongs to the almighty Todd?

But Todd isn't just a piece of meat to be objectified by drunken girls. He has a sweet, charitable side, too.

The problem with soft-top Jeeps is that anybody can unzip him and get in. One time, I found a homeless man sleeping in Todd.

"Just give me another five minutes," he said after I woke him.

"I have to go to work, so if you don't mind..." I said.

"My bad. My bad. You got a good car here."

The homeless guy sat up and started taking the loose change out of Todd's cup holder.

"Are you seriously stealing my change?" I asked him.

"Yeah. Todd would've wanted it that way," he retorted, and then he took the change and left.

Who am I to argue with logic like that?

Over the years, I've acquired a million stories like these. Todd, in a weird way, has become part of my identity. Which is why it will be so hard to give him away. Through no fault of Todd's own, a growing family and need for more space has me looking for a more practical car. It breaks my heart.

This weekend, I'll be sending out invitations to Todd's going-away party. Friends, family, music, food and drink will celebrate Todd, who will sit center stage, parked in the middle of my backyard, surrounded by buckets of sudsy, soapy water and huge sponges so that everyone who loves him can wash him down one last time. I also will have a box for folks to write down their favorite Todd memories. We will read them aloud by the glow of Todd's headlights as the sun goes down.

A small part of me hopes the homeless man from Baltimore reads this column, makes his way to my backyard and reads aloud his story of the night spent in Todd.

The Search for the Perfect Pet

"What the (expletive) is that?" screeched the man laying down my new carpet, as he danced around the room, trying to escape the creature sniffing his shoes.

"That's just my rabbit," I said.

"Sorry, ma'am, but that is no rabbit."

It's rarely love at first sight when folks meet my 18-pound gray-haired Flemish giant, Pig. With free rein of my house, Pig often catches unsuspecting people off-guard -- especially those guests who aren't forewarned about Pig's favorite hiding spot, behind the toilet, and meet Pig when he pops up between their legs. There have been a few startled screams from the bathroom. One friend even ran out with her pants around her ankles.

I really ought to put a warning sign on the door.

"He's perfectly harmless," I told the carpet man.

"Harmless?" he scoffed. "Aren't you afraid that monster will eat your baby?"

Funny he'd mention that.

A few years ago, my husband and I were going through that odd nesting phase couples experience when talk of having children is on the table but the act of doing so is still a ways off. We were looking for something to fill the void -- something to, well, practice on. (Sorry, PETA.) So we began searching for the perfect pet, an animal with fewer needs than a dog but one that wouldn't be restricted to a cage.

We settled on becoming proud parents to a potbellied pig. That is, until I read -- on a pig advocacy site emphasizing the importance of bringing a pig into the right type of home -- a harrowing article about new parents whose jealous pig had sneaked into their nursery, lowered the crib gate and eaten their baby. Yes, you read right; the pig ate the baby.

We decided, instead, to get a giant rabbit and name him Pig. Close enough.

As first-time pet parents, we marveled over the rabbit, whom we affectionately referred to as our firstborn. In no time, we transformed into those snarky parents everyone hates.

Aww, your rabbit eats carrots and hay? How adorably bourgeois. No, Pig doesn't feel as if he has to conform to bunny stereotypes. Rather, he dines on organic strawberries and the occasional baseboard molding.

We took videos of Pig pulling pillows off the couch to create obstacle courses for himself; made Facebook status updates about his litter box training; laughed heartily as Pig jumped back in fear during his daily discovery of his arch-nemesis, a bench that hasn't moved from its spot since before Pig was brought home; and took the parenting duties of our firstborn very seriously, ensuring that he came on command and made good choices when we told him to.

The week I brought home my newborn son, I posted photos on Facebook of him lying next to his furry big brother. Pig tripled my son's weight and size. Facebook friends and Facebook fans alike flooded me with messages, needing to know how Pig was coping with the transition of having a new baby in the house -- not how I was doing, just how Pig was.

Truthfully, Pig's struggled with the change. When I sing to my baby, Pig chews on curtains, demanding attention. When I'm breast-feeding, Pig nuzzles his face under my feet, forcing a head rub. Every time I'm in the nursery, Pig makes a mad dash to under the crib, and when I try to entice him out, Pig stamps his foot, snorts and breaks into a full-blown temper tantrum. I half expect him to yell "you don't love me anymore!" and run away to the next-door neighbors as I did when my mom brought my little brother home.

But for as jealous as Pig gets, he's become very protective of his little brother. Every time my son cries, Pig comes running to check on him and waits by the foot of the bed, couch or changing table, looking up attentively, until the crying stops. Pig may not have the jaw strength to eat my baby, like his namesake, but he also doesn't have the temperament.

"Only place I'd want a giant rabbit is in my stew pot," the carpet man said. As if he understood, Pig began chewing on the cuff of the man's jeans. The carpet man squealed.

"Pig, make good choices," I sang. The carpet man's jaw dropped as my well-trained rabbit hopped away from the man and out of the bedroom.

Pig made a good choice, and I smiled at my furry firstborn, one of the best choices I've ever made.

Breaking Up With Matt Damon

Dear Matt Damon,

I think it's time we see other people.

Admit it; we've grown apart, and the chasm between us is just too big to bridge. I'm sorry, but you must have sensed this was coming. We both know it's time I find a new celebrity crush.

We had a good run, didn't we? Like those times you were in a bunch of Jason Bourne movies and then I went out and saw those

Bourne movies. Remember that? And then there was that time you won an Oscar and I watched you win it. Remember? Good times.

I never thought it would end like this. Our common foundation seemed so strong. You are a writer. I am a writer. Your mom's a teacher. My dad's a teacher. You went to Harvard. I went to a university that someone once referred to as the Harvard of Ohio state schools. How could we go wrong?

I'll never forget when you first became my celebrity crush. You were an unknown playing an anti-Semite in "School Ties." I was a young Jewess who saw past your questionable acting roles. And I like to think you felt safe and comforted in our relationship, because we came together before "Good Will Hunting" made you into a household name.

Sure, we've had our rough patches. I never thought we'd recover from the embarrassment inflicted after a poster of you next to my bed prompted a series of lectures about the birds and the bees. And I somehow found a way to forgive your ridiculous blond hair in "Rounders." Even after "Stuck on You," I stuck with you. And to be fair, it's not as if I was always the perfect crusher. We can't ignore those few years when Heath Ledger caught my eye and I, shamefully, was less than faithful to you. James McAvoy even turned my head once or twice. But I always came back.

This breakup must come as a shock. And believe me; I don't take this decision lightly. You have been my main imaginary squeeze for more than half my life, since I was 14 and scribbling Katiedid Damon in hearts on my Trapper Keeper.

It's not you. It's me.

I don't want you to think you've done anything wrong. It's not because you've gotten older and puffier, though that is probably what I'll tell my friends. You may not be the swinging bachelor of your youth, but even as your personal life evolved, it only solidified my crush. I felt closer to you when you got married, because you met your wife in a bar and I, as you know, frequent bars. Another common interest! When your children came along, I enjoyed watching "E! News" and seeing pictures of you being a doting dad. We could have overcome anything you threw at me. But now I'm the one who has changed.

I started feeling the distance between us when I got pregnant. The joy in a celebrity crush is imagining yourself in a life very different from your own, in love with someone very different from the person you're in love with. The fantasy flourishes in the contrasts, and our lives are starting to parallel.

Not to get too gross or anything, but I married a pretty dang handsome dude, who also happens to be a word nerd and the son of a teacher, just like you. And now, with the new addition to our family, he, too, is a loving daddy.

Do you see the fundamental problem? I can't crush on what I have.

I want you to know, there is no third party. It's not as if I'm not cheating on you with Justin Bieber now that he's single. C'mon, give me credit; I have taste. And that's not what this is about. Sure, friends have suggested Ryan Gosling or Chris Hemsworth as rebound crushes, but I don't know.

For now, I will just watch "The Informant" on a loop and try to only remember you as that puffy, flabby guy with a silly mustache and a fake nose. And maybe, in time, I will completely get over you and find my new celebrity crush, someone who represents the antithesis of you. If you know of any illiterate, womanizing celebrities who like to dropkick babies, can you give them my number?

I hope we still can be friends.

Love,

Katiedid

Hairy Parenting

"It's as if your son has done a complete 180."

And so it begins. My life as a parent in principals' offices. The years of worrying about whether my child is being bullied or, in this case, bullying. Not even 2 1/2 and my son is already a troublemaker.

Previously, teachers had only commented on my toddler's sweetness. He didn't hit, shove or bite. He was the perfect little man. Until now.

My sweet angel had turned into a monster, terrorizing classmates by pulling their hair.

When the teacher told me of his behavior, images of my child bringing havoc, hysteria and hair-pulling to his classroom flashed through my mind. Sweet Angel gnashing his teeth. Sweet Angel roaring aloud. Sweet Angel threatening to eat the other children. No, wait. That's "Where the Wild Things Are."

73

Mustn't get carried away.

He's just acting his age, right? I know my son better than anyone, and he's a sweetie. I mean, sure, he can be a tad sneaky. A tad manipulative. And he can fake a smile or frown better than anyone. And he does have a strange affinity for rubber ducks. Oh, no, he's Macaulay Culkin in "The Good Son"!

Enough! Deep breaths. I sought out a rational explanation.

"Not that I want to *that* parent who says it's not her kid's fault," I heard myself saying, "but are you sure it was my kid's fault?" The teacher just looked at me.

Right.

Since becoming a mom, I've carried on most days without much thought to how I am parenting. It just happens, ticking along in step with time. But then there are moments that make me step back and re-evaluate what kind of parent I want to be. This was one of those moments.

Last month, I was faced with another moment. When I was shopping for new sneakers for my son, he fell in love with a pair of pink sparkly shoes. Rather than buy them, I steered my toddler in the direction of the black and red gender-appropriate kicks. It's weighed heavily on my heart ever since. He loves his new shoes, but do I really want to be the kind of parent who enforces such gender nonsense?

Here I was again, at the precipice of setting a parenting precedent. I wanted to get it right this time.

Was I truly determined to be the not-my-child's-fault parent? Maybe. If he's truly innocent and I'm being an advocate for my child, then absolutely. But there is a fine line between advocacy and raising your son to become one of the entitled, irresponsible men coerced into taking a paternity test on "Maury." "Sweet Angel, you ARE the father."

Perhaps I should avoid taking a stance on fault and rather move forward, strictly enforcing the must-do's. Clearly defining rules of right and wrong. But there is something powerful in giving the freedom to your child to find his own personal boundaries and decide what constitutes good and bad by learning from consequences of his own actions. Like, for me, skiing, tequila and sleeping under the stars are good. When all done together in a single evening, it's very, very bad.

I often think the hardest part of parenting is deciding what truly bothers you. Not society, you. I, for one, love bratty kids. Always have. I love kids who think for themselves. Question authority. Test boundaries. You can't stir minds, innovate or change the world without being a tad naughty. Bratty kids talk back because they have something clever to say. It's my job as a parent to remember that when I'm picking my son up from the principal's office. It's also my job to make sure my kid doesn't go from bratty to just plain obnoxious.

Pulling hair is obnoxious.

After a few days of daily updates on my son's maniacal hair-pulling madness, I still didn't have the answer for how to parent this turn in my child's behavior. I was about to ask for advice, when one of his teachers pulled me aside.

"So, we may have made a mistake. We watched your son closely, and he's not being aggressive. He's not even trying to pull the girls' hair; he just wants to style it."

My son isn't a monster. He's a hairdresser.

I bought him an Elsa hat with a long blond braid so he can participate in the hair play. I may be a slow learner, but I learn.

Cookie Batter Up!

I love going to baseball games. That's not to say I love baseball. I like baseball. I respect baseball. I admire the game, the athleticism, the calculations, the mind play, but that's not why I go to games. I go for the nachos.

I'm kidding. (I'm not kidding.) I go for more than just the nachos. (They also have soft pretzels.) I go for the atmosphere.

I live for those perfect summer evenings, when the sun is warm on your face and the light zephyr cools you down, when the orange moon rises over the outfield stands and the evening is thick with screaming children, baseball gloves in tow. I love standing up for the wave, belting out the national anthem and attempting to pelt poor players with popcorn, which inevitably rains on the fans one row below mine, causing an uncomfortable grudge for the duration of the game.

Sometimes, if I'm really lucky, a fight will break out -- among the players, not between me and the row in front. (Usually.) There is something primal and absurdly awesome about a good baseball fight.

75

Unlike hockey or football, the players have to run great distances -- from home plate and the dugout and even the bullpen to the mound -- just for the opportunity to throw a punch. And because it takes so long to get there, the fight is often broken up before it begins, resulting in a hilarious horde filled with unrequited aggression and pretend anger, featuring empty threats and profane gestures.

Sidebar: High schools should look into implementing a 50-yard dash before students are allowed to tackle one another in the hallways. That would not only help prevent fights but also enhance physical fitness in the absence of gym class. It's a win-win.

No matter which stadium you attend or which team you are watching, with a hot dog (tofu dog) in one hand and a large cola (beer) in the other, the atmosphere is what feels like home. OK, not really. I don't associate my physical abode with peanut shells crushed on the floor. And I think I'd be really freaked out if someone pointed at me with a foot-long finger made of foam, but you get what I'm saying. It's joy in the form of bleachers. The perfect diamond. I mean, they sell soft serve in a mini baseball cap. In a cap, people!

My elder cousin Jeff, whom I idolized growing up, is responsible for my love of going to games. A baseball fanatic, he taught me how to fill in a score chart and taught me the rules. He'd make mad dashes for refills on snacks, only to drill me on the play-by-play of everything that had occurred in his absence. I associate attending baseball games with the kind of nostalgia that I feel when buying candy cigarettes from the ice cream man or wearing a heavy-metal shirt under my pantsuit.

Baseball has always been part of my life.

Recently, in a knee-jerk reaction to becoming a father, my husband bought season tickets. His statement to the world that parenthood would not change us. Adorable. Laughable. Inaccurate. But hey, it's cheaper than buying a two-seater convertible.

Baseball games are now spent preoccupying a toddler. Chasing after him, throwing a ball with him, an endless cycle of cars and crayons and snacks and books -- anything to keep his bottom in his seat. It's rough. The atmosphere cannot be experienced, the alcohol not properly consumed, the wave not waved when engaged in toddler entertaining.

Here's the odd thing. My kid loves baseball. Not going to the games but rather the actual game. Free from the distraction of screaming fans, fried foods and rogue beach balls, he can stand in front of the television and watch the game for hours. He loves it so much that when he entered an older class at day care and was instructed to say a prayer before his snack for the first time, he clapped out a baseball cheer.

I've learned something from watching my son's enthrallment with the game. It turns out that the players have names. And positions. And averages. Turns out baseball isn't only about nachos. (Just mostly.) Though I knew that, somewhere between sunflower seeds and Cracker Jack boxes, I'd forgotten.

Going into the postseason, I'm excited to say I know a thing or two. Touchdown!

Starbucks' Holiday Drinks

Hi, my name is Katiedid Langrock, and I'm a Starbucks-aholic. Well, not really. I merely lose all self-control and self-worth during the season of Starbucks' festive specialty holiday hot drinks. That's all.

Not to worry, I've decided this year is the year I will kick the coffee habit. No, for real this time. Not like the past 10 years. Do they sell a patch that quells the cravings for eggnog latte?

What is it about the specialty holiday drinks that makes me develop an annual abusive relationship with Starbucks? I know they are bad for me. I know the relationship is toxic. Every year, I tell myself that this is the year that I will control the peppermint mocha. The peppermint mocha will not control me! But then this year, like every other, I came crawling back into the relationship.

It all starts off so innocently with the autumn release of the pumpkin spice latte, the perfect welcome wagon to cooler weather. I tell myself that festive drinks and I can be friends -- or at least acquaintances who coexist. They don't need me, and I don't need them. But then, as food porn photos of pumpkin lattes pop up on social media, my obsession takes hold. I need one! It needs me to need one. How can you be sure it is autumn until you have warm gourd-infused espresso in your happy belly? You can't! It's impossible. I become convinced that the world would stop spinning on its axis if I did not purchase at least one grande. I order it -- for science.

When it comes to the pumpkin spice latte, I'm usually one and done. But don't be fooled. Pumpkin spice latte is the gateway drug into all other specialty holiday drinks.

Most years, by November, I still feel strong. I haven't yet realized that the seeds of my addiction have been planted. I don't recognize that headaches are slowly popping up when I go too long without caffeine. I don't pay attention to my chronic scratching of my left elbow when I don't have a white cardboard coffee cup in my hand. Once the chalkboard menus are rewritten for winter, I am an instant rehab candidate. So many options! So few winter months!

It's a problem -- not just to my wallet or to my health but because this daily Starbucks visit endangers the core of my very being. You see, the specialty holiday coffee -- if you can call it coffee -- it, it changes me. It's as if my chemical makeup alters. My usual sunny and easygoing disposition flares into easy and immediate rage. The only thing that can quell the fury is a sip of a hot sugary beverage loaded with empty calories. And then another. And another. I'm just not myself when I do the brew.

A few weeks ago, I ordered my drug of choice, the salted caramel mocha, in a Starbucks drive-thru. When I got to work, I realized I accidentally had been given plain drip coffee. The horror! I immediately drove back to the coffeehouse and demanded to speak with a manager. Who could allow such poor workmanship from her employees?! While I waited for the manager to come out and accept my tongue-lashing, I was given the proper drink to sip on. By the time the manager arrived, my tummy was warm, happy and full of salty, chocolaty goodness. I had nothing but praises to offer. But it was a close call.

After my near psycho incident, I decided once and for all that this will be the year I break free from my addiction. If I need a warm drink to fight the cold, I will order a regular drip coffee. It will be better on my wallet, on my scale and on my emotional well-being. This year, I will walk away from Starbucks' specialty holiday drinks season with my sanity in tact.

I entered my local Starbucks for the first time this year, mentally prepared to order my black coffee. But something scribbled on the chalkboard menu caught my eye. What was this? Caramel flan latte! A new specialty holiday drink? I had to have it. What if the Earth would stop spinning on its axis if I didn't at least try the caramel flan latte? I ordered the coffee. I mean, really, what harm could one drink do?

The Katydid Hunter

"I'm so excited to finally get you on the phone. I've been dying to meet you," said a potential consulting client. "My son and I are obsessed with katydids."

I was named after the katydid, a long insect that looks like the love child of a grasshopper and a mantis. Most people aren't familiar with katydids, so anytime I meet someone who shares my affection for the bug, I'm over the moon.

"I approve of your obsession! How'd that happen?" I asked.

"My son had to find a katydid in the wild for a science project. We named him Harvey."

"I love it!" I exclaimed, thinking this caller might just be my soul mate.

"We really fell in love with Harvey. Do you think I'm weird?"

"Of course not," I said. And I meant it.

"I cried more when that bug died than I did when my dog died. Now you must think I'm weird."

"Not at all," I said. But I didn't quite mean it.

"Probably even more than when my mom died..."

Uh-oh.

"...And I really loved my mom."

Psycho alert. Psycho alert.

"We could tell Harvey was getting sick. We didn't know what to feed him."

"You should've let him back in the wild," I said.

"Never!" yelled my potential client.

Whoa. Where's the fire, angrypants?

"I loved him. Would you just throw something you love back into the wild?"

Uh, yeah.

"I guess not," I said.

"I feel sorry for you," she said. "You must not know real love."

Right. That must be it.

"Yep. That must be it."

"Harvey was brown with a bit of green. They come in both colors, you know."

Don't engage. You don't want this person as a client anyway. Hang up the phone.

"We actually come in lots of colors," I heard myself saying against my better judgment. "We come in bright pink and with yellow stripes and orange--"

"No, they don't!"

Abort call. Abort! Abort!

"OK. Sorry. I guess I'm mistaken," I said. "So look, I really have to get going."

Good girl. Now hang up the phone.

"Once Harvey died, we knew we could never be without. Our house needs a katydid."

"What do you mean by you could never be without?" I couldn't help asking.

t's not my fault; I had to engage! When you're named after a bug, you grow a sort of kinship to it. I identify with my totem insect, and if katydids are being harmed, I have to know about it. I have to fix it. I have to save them!

"My son and I take hikes in the woods, hunting katydids. They're a North American treasure, you know."

Hunting?

"But we can't take the heartache of growing attached, only to have it die in a few months like Harvey did, so now we put them in a jar without air holes."

I'd like to put you in a jar without air holes!

"This way, they're dead in a few days, and we don't get heartbroken."

It's not worth it. She's crazy. Don't engage!

"How often do you hunt katydids?" The words were sprinting out of my mouth.

"At least every weekend," she said, "and most Wednesdays."

"What?!" I screamed. "Murderer! You're committing katydid genocide!"

No, no, no. Shut up. Stop talking.

"I am not a murderer. We love katydids."

"You don't love katydids. If you loved them, you'd let them stay in their natural habitat," I yelled, "which, by the way, includes every continent except for Antarctica. They are not even close to a North American treasure!"

My co-workers stopped what they were doing to stare at me yelling into the phone. But I wasn't stopping. Not on your life!

"And I was not mistaken; we do come in hot pink. And stripes. And spikes. And some look more like leaves. And some look more like twigs. And before you go around killing off my people, perhaps you could learn a little more about us!"

I breathed heavily into the phone. I was ready for a fight. I wanted one.

On the other end of the phone was silence. And then:

"You know you're not a bug, right?" she asked. "I think you might be a little unbalanced."

It's a sad day when you realize that your own dose of craziness has surpassed that of an angry katydid killer lady. A sad day indeed.

That New Car Smell

In preparation for the new baby, I had my car detailed. And by detailed, I mean scrubbed down to an inch of its life.

I refuse to believe it's an exaggeration to say that never in the history of vehicles has there ever been one in such need of a hose-down. Move over, mud-wrestling monster trucks and creepy neighbor's van, which now houses an ex-boyfriend, his Spam obsession and your shared-custody harem of hairless rats. You had nothing on my Subaru. Even the dusty wagons on the Oregon Trail got a nice wash while crossing the river at the end.

Morning drop-offs at preschool had left my poor car blanketed in Goldfish, Cheerios and some sticky substance that was certainly made from peanut butter and the plague. Too busy to clean when my toddler spilled juice, I would throw a blanket over it. If my kid spilled milk on the blanket, I'd simply cover the blanket with a sweater.

If people at the Centers for Disease Control and Prevention had taken a ride in my car, they would most certainly have been placed under quarantine. Which is why, before subjecting a new baby to fuzzy cereal bars and smallpox, I shelled out $150 to give my car a thorough top-to-bottom washing.

About 3 1/2 hours later, my car came out sparkling. It smelled of soap. It shined like the sun. I took my son for a drive. Showed off the stainless seats to my neighbors. It was like a brand-new car. And I thought that this was the best $150 I had ever spent.

Then I let the car sit for the weekend.

When I opened the door to drive to work Monday morning, my car reeked. The most foul of foul stenches. A soul-crushing blow to the olfactory system.

Is this some kind of prank?

I thought back to my college days, when my friends and I had a prank war going with the boys down the hall. It all began innocently enough. We taped tampons to their doors. They stole the alcohol from our room. We left an anonymous message with the RA so they would get in trouble for having liquor that was actually ours. It was all in great fun -- especially when we began upping the ante.

One time, our friends fastened a bucket of water to our doorway, so when my roommate walked through the door, 2 gallons of water spilled on her head. Sadly, she was carrying her laptop at the time, which drowned in the prank juice, never to be started again. Our retaliation had to be strong. We thought long and hard about what would make the boys suffer.

One of our guy friends had recently begun dating a new girl. While we watched him scrub the room he shared in preparation for a date with his new fling, we came up with the perfect revenge. It was so simple. So easy. So potent.

That night, we returned from the dining hall with a glass of milk, sneaked into the boys' room and hid the milk behind their dresser. It took a week for the milk to have a real effect, but soon their room began to stink. And then it reeked. And then it was unforgiving.

We watched as these poor boys washed everything in their room, trying to find the source of the stench. They did their laundry. Once. Twice. Three times. Cleaned the sheets. Bleached their minifridge. Washed the floors. Febrezed the curtains. Doused the dorm room in cologne. And still the stench lingered.

That is, until we decided the boys had suffered enough and told them about the milk hiding behind their dresser.

I love a good prank war.

After making such a big deal out of my newly cleaned car, I was confident some friend would come forward and admit to the wrongdoing she had committed on my Subaru. A stink bomb, perhaps? But after a week of lingering stench and no loved ones raising their hands, I called the carwash.

"Any idea as to why my car smells so awful after going to your carwash?" I asked the manager.

"Have you looked to see if any food fell under the seat?"

And there it was -- my toddler's sippy cup, full of solidified milk. Gross.

Jeep Bed

I believe in soul mates.

A soul mate is someone who understands you and your needs implicitly, who can switch gears when you do, who takes you on adventures, who quite simply blows your hair back. I am one of those lucky people to have found my soul mate. And did I mention he has a great body?

My husband, you ask? Ha-ha, adorable. And no.

I'm talking about Todd, my two-door soft-top Jeep Wrangler. Don't worry; the husband knows about Todd and has come to terms with our extramarital love affair. He even has gotten used to my gossiping to friends about taking Todd's top off and enjoying a ride. Twice. Truly, the husband has no reason to be jealous because, ultimately, I chose him. I chose our family.

Todd and I broke up almost exactly three years ago, after I had my son. Though the husband could embrace Todd into our lives, I'm guessing Child Protective Services would have looked down on a sunburned 1-month-old's being wind-lashed in the back seat as we barreled down the highway, topless, doorless and free. Giving up Todd felt as if I was giving up a part of myself.

There are a bajillion articles (yes, that's the actual number) written for new parents to encourage them not to lose themselves in their new role as Mommy or Daddy. But some hobbies just have to go for practical reasons, such as raising rabid wolverines, becoming an amateur indoor pyrotechnics artist and driving a car that you've always secretly wanted to test the rollover bar on. It was time to give up my more reckless interests for responsible ones. Tears were shed as Todd was traded in for a family-friendly crossover utility vehicle.

Sometimes I think I see him driving in front of me, the sunlight bouncing off his taillights into my eyes. And I wonder whether he, like Clint Eastwood hanging the charm on his rearview mirror at the end of "The Bridges of Madison County," is beckoning me to follow him. Oh, Meryl Streep and I have so much in common -- and not just our shared Oscar nominations and raw beauty and talent. We both know what it's like to choose our children over our soul mates.

Like many parents, I actively encourage my personal interests and have been pointing out Jeeps to my son since before he could hold up his own head. So when I saw that Little Tikes had come out with a toddler Jeep bed, owning it became my obsession. And by owning it, I mean *my* owning it. Let's be clear; this bed would be for me under the guise of being for my son.

For nearly a year, I fantasized about that Jeep bed, about turning on the bed's headlights and dome light -- which actually work! -- as I read my son his bedtime stories. Naturally, my son would feel a little scared his first few nights out of the crib. I would tell him, *No worries, son. I'm happy to sleep in bed with you.* I would say, *Just for tonight.* But I wouldn't mean it.

In preparation for the new arrival, I decorated my son's room so the Jeep bed would feel at home. Stars were placed on the ceiling. Dead batteries in the moon nightlight were replaced. A tent was set up in the corner of the room. The room took the shape of the great outdoors as I waited patiently for my son to outgrow his crib.

And then it happened. My son climbed out of his crib for the first time. That very thing that had terrified me for so long -- the broken bones, the concussions! -- was now greeted with unadulterated glee. He climbed out! The crib is no longer safe! Hurray! We can transition him to a big-boy bed! A big-boy Jeep bed!

His first night, the bedtime routine went exactly how I had envisioned over the past year. My son and I snuggled under the covers as I read him bedtime stories by the light of the Jeep bed's headlights. The star stickers shone above us. The pitter-patter of rainfall came from the sound machine. When the stories were finished, I said, "You probably want me to sleep here because it's your first night in a new bed, huh."

"Nope!" my son announced proudly. "Leave, Mommy. Good night!"

But, but, but...

Crestfallen.

~ ~ ~

Chapter 6

Knocked Up Again?: Pregnancy Part 2

Babies, Bunnies and a Bucket of Chicken

It was a week before Easter. Suffering from an insatiable sweet tooth, my husband broke into the Easter Bunny's stash early. He unwrapped a chocolate bunny and took a bite out of its ears.

I immediately started to cry.

"What's wrong?" my husband asked.

"Why would you do that?" I asked through sobs. "You can't just bite his ears. He can feel that. You're hurting him. You have to break his neck first."

Convinced I was messing with him, as I so often am, my husband took another bite of the chocolate ears.

"Stop!" I cried, my face now wet with tears. "Don't you care? Break his neck before you hurt him any more! Stop being a monster!"

My husband, one eyebrow slightly raised, broke off the head of the hollow chocolate bunny. I inhaled a deep breath of relief. My husband then came over to hug me, laughing, as he continued to gnaw on the now-severed chocolate ears.

Perhaps now is a good time to mention I'm pregnant.

Other than relentless vomiting, there were not many typical pregnancy stereotypes that plagued my first pregnancy, but shedding tears over nonsense was one of them. More than three years ago, when I was pregnant with my son and not yet telling people, I went to dinner with friends. We were deciding on which dessert to share, and no one was interested in the one that appealed to me. But then the waiter came out with free sorbet, the dessert I had been eyeing, for everyone at our table -- an apology for making us wait to be seated after our reservation time. It was a magical moment.

"It's exactly what I wanted," I cried, trying to hide the tears rolling down my face. I made joyful eye contact with my husband, who looked around at our friends, terrified the jig was up. Luckily, they were still so immersed in the dessert menu they didn't take notice that their often stoic and sarcastic friend was crying over mango sorbet.

My current pregnancy has kept the tears, kept the relentless vomiting and added a whole other host of crazy. Now I understand why they say men have it rough when their wives are pregnant.

Very little food has been appetizing, so when I had a craving last week, it was a big deal.

"I want a bucket of chicken," I declared.

"You're a vegetarian," my husband offered quietly, as if reminding me, fearful pregnancy brain had wiped even that knowledge away. I glared.

"Dude! I'm starving."

"OK," he said. "I'll go to KFC."

"No. I want food from Roy Rogers."

"Roy Rogers? I'm pretty sure the nearest one is on the Pennsylvania Turnpike," which is more than 2,000 miles from where we live.

"Yeah, but you don't know that, do you?" I snapped.

My husband looked up the tiny chain of fast-food restaurants. He was right. But when he showed me the website with proof of the absurd distance, I just stared back and said, "I don't understand why you're not getting into your car right now."

Pregnancy does weird things to you. It plays tricks with your eyes. It plays tricks with your mind. I've stared longingly at a candle, licking my lips, because it looked so delicious. A candle! I've developed an obsession with smushing jelly beans between my fingers. I associate weird smells with different people for no apparent reason, and that dictates whether I want to be around them or not. My neighbor smells like pickles. A co-worker smells like recently cut grass. A friend smells like carrot juice. My pet rabbit smells, well, delicious. Maybe with a little seasoning... Gah! What's wrong with me?!

This, too, shall pass, my mom reminds me. And luckily, during both my pregnancies, the moments of both rational and irrational thought seem to pass quickly. This can be annoying when I have finally found an appetizing meal but am over it by the time the microwave dings that it's done. However, the quick change of mind has also kept me from ever biting into a bucket of chicken, a candle or my beloved rabbit.

People say that your crazy hormones are a sign that you are cooking a healthy baby and that's always something to be grateful for. Perhaps it's also a sign that this kid will be full of tricks, both in the womb and out of it. The due date is Halloween, after all.

Drinking While Pregnant

They say you shouldn't drink while pregnant, but I've developed a codependency with beer.

Ginger beer.

My mom was visiting last weekend, and during her trip, two things were brought to light. One: You are never too old to be mothered by your mother. My mom saw how sick I am with my all-day morning sickness and spent her vacation doing my dishes, going grocery shopping and watching my toddler while I took naps. Being mommied by your mommy when you, too, are a mommy is awesome. Two: Ginger beer is the only thing that makes me feel slightly human. Another gift from Mom.

Over her visit, my mom and I engaged in the world's lamest pub crawl. Dry countries, ones that don't even allow alcohol within their borders, have more exciting drink-and-dash sampler nights. We drove from store to store, looking for ginger beer, taste testing a variety of bottles and obsessing over the ingredients.

(To be read in an aggressive New York accent) *Only pure cane sugar and 100 percent fresh ginger for my girl.*

Thanks, Mom.

The most annoying thing about buying ginger beer is that the good stuff -- and I mean the really good stuff -- can be found only in liquor stores. I have never wanted to drink more than when I am pregnant. It's not that I need a drink, per se, or that I even really want a drink. It's that anytime someone tells me "no," I have to do that very thing ASAP. It's part of that whole being aversively motivated thing. You may remember this delightful disposition from your teen years. I, apparently, am still living through my adolescence. I wonder whether this means I could still run for student body president. I really think I could get the school cafeteria to start exclusively serving Pop-Tart ice-cream sandwiches and pizza tacos.

Being aversively motivated has worked great for me when sweet, kind souls have attempted to destroy my self-esteem and dreams by telling me I could never be a writer. Living in a perpetual Opposite Day didn't work out so hot when I was advised, "Don't light candles in your room. You'll burn the carpet." Nor did it work well when I was told, "Don't bring a blowup doll as your date to prom. People will think you're weird."

(Psst, remind me to tell you the tales of the carpet fire and the latex prom date. It's some pretty juicy stuff.)

My friends in college always made fun of me because if I was asked to write a five-page paper arguing why bathing in poison ivy is bad, I'd write a 20-page paper about why a soak in the toxic plant is rejuvenating -- just because *you can't tell me what to do!* I would quadruple the workload solely to be defiant. I'm not very smart.

I'm also not a very big drinker. I will drink socially, but let's be honest. I have a toddler. When am I ever social? It's being told I'm not allowed to drink that makes me want to go all Ernest Hemingway. Having to go into a liquor store to buy my virgin tummy-beer feels decidedly obedient -- a word I removed from my wedding vows and general vocabulary.

It is probably worth mentioning at this time that I do not intend to drink during this pregnancy, nor did I drink after I found out about my first pregnancy. There was that one time I was in my friend's wedding at eight months and I walked down the aisle sipping from a flask, but that was only because we had just been given the flasks as bridesmaid gifts, and if you've ever experienced Philadelphia in July, you'll understand why I needed the water inside.

Today I had my 16-week checkup, and despite the fact that I continue to vomit a couple of times a day, my doctor was very happy to see I had put on "one good pound" since getting pregnant. The scale actually showed I had put on three. I'm sure I have the ginger beer to thank for this small victory. It's just like what Mom tells you when you first go off to college: Drinking packs on the pounds, so stay away from frat parties. And bars. And frat boys. And underage drinking in your dorms. And really any place where there is booze. Or boys. Especially boys wearing hats with Greek letters.

Cheers.

Peace. Love. Mope.

While in the playground area of a fair in the back hills, I came across two women wearing boho apparel and flowers in their hair. Their conversation was slightly less hippie-dippy than their attire.

"You're so-o-o-o skinny," said the first lady

"No, you're so skinny," replied her friend.

"No, you are. I look like I'm five months pregnant."

"Well, how far along are you now?"

"Only seven months."

Then the ladies proceeded to talk about the diets they are on to stay skinny throughout their pregnancies.

I hate fake hippies.

The negativity. The entitlement. The affluence. The ignorance. The total and unabashed posing and self-importance. As if wearing a $200 flower crown magically transforms the person from who she truly is to an earth-loving, chakra-aligning, Zen-achieving sprite. There are many festivals that cater to the faux free spirit, and last weekend, I found myself at one of them.

I had read about the tiny community fair online. After pushing my son's stroller up an incredibly steep dirt hill, I wiped sweat from my brow and looked down on a small canyon lined with tents and a stage.

Glee. Glee is what I felt. It looked like the markets I used to attend weekly in Australia. I love real hippies. I come from their stock, and though I don't live as one -- nor do I pretend to -- I enjoy bearing witness to it, experiencing that world and magic firsthand, if only for a little bit. Down in the canyon, I expected to find kooky craftsmen and ladies lost in song. I expected stoners and old folks with amazing stories. I expected beautiful young people and vegans and naturists. I expected shoppers. And sellers. And musicians. And poets. And dreamers.

I was wrong. Rather than lovers, there was petty one-upmanship. Rather than hemp dresses, there was haute couture. Rather than potheads, I'm pretty sure everyone was on crystal meth. With real crystals in them. Like, basically blood diamond meth. A drunk woman stumbled up to my toddler and asked to pick him up. When he hid behind my legs, she slurred, "Is he stupid? Your kid will never be a model!"

John and Yoko would be so proud.

That's not to say the festival was void of any authenticity. My son and I listened to wonderful live music while we sipped on coconuts, our feet bare in the grass. There was a smattering of those hairy, beautiful bohemians I love, and there were a decent number of folks who came to enjoy the event without treating it like a costume party.

The danger with having two very different groups of people with opposing ideologies pretending to be the same is that inevitably, one group begins to win out and influence the other.

After a few hours, my son and I had had enough, and we began the long and hot trek back to my car. My son was asleep and I was drenched in sweat by the time we reached it, only to find a police car's lights whirling as a cop was writing me a parking ticket.

"Hey!" I yelled out. The cop looked up as I ran up to him. "Why are you writing me a ticket?"

"Because you're parked directly under a 'no parking' sign," the cop said, pointing to it.

Something came over me. I -- who am always respectful, if not fearful, of cops -- lost my cool. I could blame the heat. Or my fatigue. Or pregnancy. But it felt like something else entirely. I began arguing with the cop, giving a laundry list of overly entitled reasons I didn't deserve the ticket despite my obvious negligence. Eventually, the cop took pity on me -- or perhaps just tired of my tirade -- and ripped up the ticket.

It was only then that I realized the car was not mine.

It didn't even look like my car. The Lexus only shared a similar shade of gold as my Subaru, which was parked perfectly legally a few cars down. I looked at the Lexus parked under the "no parking" sign and shuddered. The festival of faux free spirits had rubbed off on me.

Mortified, I walked to my car and drove directly to get ice cream. At least I wouldn't be influenced by the pregnancy diet.

Food Diary of a Mad Pregnant Lady

2:45 a.m.: Wake up starving.

2:46 a.m.: Convince yourself you can go back to sleep.

2:51 a.m.: Accept that there will be no sleep. Decide that if that obnoxious freak David Blaine can fast for 44 days, you can make it until sunrise.

2:52 a.m.: Feel bad for calling David Blaine a freak.

2:57 a.m.: Get a yogurt and slowly indulge on the couch, embracing every delectable lick of the spoon. Resolve you were right; David Blaine is a freak. Food is awesome.

3:30 a.m.: Wake up with heartburn.

7:20 a.m.: Make cereal for breakfast.

7:21 a.m.: Realize you somehow have forgotten to put on a shirt.

7:30 a.m.: Find a shirt that actually fits around the growing bump and then leave. No time to eat.

8:04 a.m.: Remind yourself that when you're pregnant, the hungrier you get the dumber you become and the worse food sounds. Avoid the starvation cycle. Even the folks in the human centipede have to eat.

8:05 a.m.: Pull in to the Starbucks drive-thru. Decide there is nothing on the menu that looks good. You're too late. Ask the barista for a caffeine-free drink.

8:15 a.m.: A co-worker sees you sipping on a green tea latte and says, "You know there's a lot of caffeine in that." Throw the drink away. Tell yourself you feel full.

8:23 a.m.: Go to the work refrigerator. Stare at options, none of which is appetizing.

8:26 a.m.: Close the fridge door and notice the large magnet of a condom on the door. Scrawled across the condom are the words "Just wear it." Think the condom is taunting you. It whispers, "If you'd only listened to me, you could eat everything in this fridge. Just wear it."

8:27 a.m.: Look around the kitchen, curious about whether anyone read your crazy thoughts about the condom magnet's talking to you.

8:28 a.m.: Realize that looking around to see whether any co-worker read your thoughts makes you even crazier. Promptly walk away from the fridge.

9:00 a.m.: Start looking up places to eat lunch, trying to find something (anything!) that sounds appealing.

9:45 a.m.: Co-worker asks whether you're going to the 10 o'clock meeting. Scream, "Can't you see I'm busy?!" Show co-worker the 50 open tabs on your computer, all of food menus. Co-worker slinks away.

9:46 a.m.: Go to the bathroom to put some cold water on your hangry face. Notice that your shirt is on inside out. Fix your shirt. Spot some crusted food on the shirt from dinner last week. Remember the meal fondly. Wonder whether it would be weird to lick your shirt just for a taste. Decide that yes, yes, that would be weird. Beyond weird. Consider again, but would it really?

9:47 a.m.: Decide to turn your shirt inside out again so you are not tempted.

10:30 a.m.: Enlist a new co-worker to find a meal that you would want to eat.

10:35 a.m.: As a joke, she suggests pumpkin bisque and raspberry pie. Start to cry. It sounds so beautiful. Yes, that is what you want for food. Right now. Nothing else will do. Co-workers remind you it is the middle of summer. Pumpkin bisque isn't even easily accessible in the winter months. Yell at your co-workers for taunting you with unavailable soup, declaring they are "worse than the condom magnet!" Watch as the co-workers stare back, blinking. Confused.

10:40 a.m.: Call co-worker friends whom you haven't yelled at and enlist them for help,in finding pumpkin soup and raspberry pie. Manage to bite your tongue when a friend asks whether raspberry pie is even a thing. You've alienated nearly everyone else this morning. You need her.

2:30 p.m.: Realize you have just spent four hours searching online for pumpkin bisque and have not done any work. You can't formulate sentences. The baby must be eating your brain.

2:35 p.m.: Drive to the cafe across the street and let the cashier pick a meal for you.

3:00 p.m.: Experience heartburn from scarfing down the deeply unsatisfying meal.

5:00 p.m.: Pack to go home. Notice something shiny in desk.

5:01 p.m.: Pull out an old can of soup. It's pumpkin bisque.

5:10 p.m.: Consider bringing the soup home for dinner, but now that you've eaten, pumpkin soup sounds disgusting.

5:15 p.m.: Pass the fridge on the way out. Grab the condom magnet off the door and throw it in the trash.

6:30 p.m.: Aren't hungry for dinner because of late lunch.

2:45 a.m.: Wake up starving.

The Goliath Changing Table

My baby-to-be's nursery is more akin to a closet. Essentially, when you step into the room, the next step you walk through a window. Great for her teenage years when she wants to sneak out. Not so great for babyhood when her room must fit a mountain of please-stop-crying newborn necessities. Ironically, the small nursery's closet is the only place that can accommodate a dresser -- a tall, skinny dresser. It's the "Sideways Stories From Wayside

92

School" of dressers. It doesn't need to be harnessed to the wall in case of an earthquake; it needs to be harnessed just in case a garbage truck drives down the street or a large bird flies overhead.

The tall-dresser-in-the-closet scenario caused an interesting dilemma when it came to the need for a changing table. My son never used one because we strapped his changing pad to his dresser -- his low, long dresser. No baby could be changed on top of my to-be-daughter's Lurch Addams of dressers. A changing table would have to be purchased -- a compact tiny one that could fit into the room. Is there such a thing as a Murphy changing table? Because if I could just pull one out of the wall, that would be great.

Last weekend, my neighborhood held a huge yard sale. I live in a very kid-friendly area, so I had high expectations that I would see my fair share of changing table options during the sale. My expectations went unmet. Almost.

A map was handed out to all of the yard sale participants, stating which items would be sold at which houses. One -- and only one -- house was selling a changing table. I just knew this was the table of my dreams -- the kind that makes you feel good about wiping a butt at 3 a.m. It was an inkling. A hunch. The sale began at 8 a.m. I was at their house by 8:05.

The changing table was nowhere to be seen.

Distraught, I asked the sellers whether the changing table had been bought already. Big mistake. I should've just walked away. I should've taken it as a sign. Divine diaper intervention.

The woman slapped her forehead and said, "I knew we forgot something!" Then she sent her husband to get it. The table must've been in the bowels of the garage, because he came back 20 minutes later, covered in sweat and dirt and wheezing. Wheezing because he had just hauled the Goliath of changing tables. This hunk of furniture is probably bigger than the entire nursery. No way, no how could it fit.

I was consumed by guilt. Could I just walk away after this man lugged out his changing monolith for me? I decided yes -- yes, I could. That's when he started to cry.

Not cry, per se, but mist. His wife rubbed his back and said, "Oh, look at him. He's getting sentimental." She explained that they had just potty trained their youngest. This changing table had served them well for nearly a decade.

"Are we sure we're done having kids?" he asked his wife. *Say no, I pleaded in my mind. Say no, and keep the table.*

"Yes."

"Are you really ready to give away all of these memories for just $15?" he asked his wife.

I saw my chance to get out of the deal.

"You shouldn't sell those memories short," I said. "Wait for someone who can pay more. It's fine."

"No," the wife said. "The changing table is yours. It just warms our heart knowing it's going to a good home."

Forehead slap.

There was one last chance to get out of buying the dresser. My car! The changing table óf Gibraltar could not fit in my car -- or any car, for that matter. But the husband offered to drive it over to my house in his truck. I was stuck.

As the hours passed, I hoped and hoped that the family from a few streets over would just rob me. These folks had my $15; maybe they would just keep the changing table and the money! My fingers were crossed.

Sadly, you just can't count on bad people anymore. Where are all the thieves? The crooks? The opportunists? With a heavy heart, my neighbor dropped off his beloved dresser and said, "Take good care of her."

I will. I'm taking her to the nicest Goodwill.

Path to Adulthood

I'm not good with titles.

I don't know the difference between "your highness" and "your majesty," between corporal and lieutenant, between serial killer and clown or between sadist and ice-cream truck driver (you know who you are!), and it just gets worse from there. Heck, I'm so bad with titles that I'm still not sure what my name is. Some call me Did. Some call me Katie. Some call me Katiedid. And a few special folks call me Willard Scott, Peaches, Wombat and Kay-Kay-the-Pretty-Bug-Dance-All-Day-Day. I'm fairly noncommittal about the whole thing. As I said, I'm not good with titles.

I especially struggle when it comes to titles that are meant to act as identifiers of who I am.

This past week, my husband and I celebrated our eighth wedding anniversary, but the titles "husband" and "wife" still make me squeamish. There is something too formal about the terms -- too ... adult. I most often refer to my husband as "the dude." And me, a wife? Nah. Shouldn't I be more domestic or more successful or more obedient or more disobedient or more ... *something* before that term applies to me? I have never once been in possession of a ball and chain, and I still don't know the difference between Mrs. and Ms. A real wife should know these things! Right?

Speaking of a title's feeling too adult, it doesn't feel as if the term "adult" applies to me, either. I still use "adult" as something to differentiate us from them -- the "them" being the adult population. Meaning not us. Meaning not me! Shouldn't I have more wisdom and fewer wisdom teeth? (I really need to get those pulled.) Sure, I've been able to vote for 15 years, but I'm more on the path *toward* adulthood than actually at the destination, right?

I have been called a writer, but I have yet to see my Oscar or Pulitzer on my mantel. I've been called an American, but I have yet to eat barbecue. I'm not a hiker, because I could never do Mount Everest. I'm not a camper, because I would die on "Naked and Afraid." Day one: death -- naked, naked death.

Even titles that I have bestowed on myself, such as backpacker, feel disingenuous. During those accumulated years I was abroad, I would salivate over other travelers' backpacks, admiring how small they were, how tightly packed -- admonishing myself for that unnecessary extra pair of socks. I bet even Shari Lewis left her socks at home when traveling, and hers sang songs! Sure, they were super-annoying, never-ending songs, but my socks can't do that. Stupid socks.

I realize that all these titles given to me -- wife, writer, Queen of the Platypuses and Popcorn Pixies -- don't feel applicable because I am waiting for some accomplishment to warrant them. When I have a solid 401(k) and come to terms with my gray hairs, I will be an adult. When I build a tent out of fig leaves, I'll be a camper. And when I can impersonate Larry the Cable Guy, I'll be American.

There is only one title that I easily embrace as an identifier: Mommy.

It didn't happen overnight. I remember wondering in those early months after my son was born whether the name "Mom" would forever feel foreign or fraudulent as all the other supposed identifiers in my life do. I was scared I would never feel right in the role, that I would never earn the title. But it came. Not after an accomplishment or achievement but slowly, over time. So slowly that I didn't even notice it, until one day it was here. I was a mom. I use the title without flinching. I feel pride when others refer to me as a mom. And I love it when my boy calls me "Mommy."

My baby girl is due next month, and our little family will be complete. What a joy it is to embark on a new adventure already feeling secure in my role, in my title. How lovely to have an identifier that can't be taken away. (Apparently, there is no such thing as a platypus popcorn pixie queen.)

I still haven't decided what I want my exact title to be -- Mom, Mama or Mommy. But as with the three variations of my first name, it doesn't matter what you call me. It simply is what I am. My name is Katie/Did/Katiedid, and I'm a mom/mommy/mama.

Epidural Take 2

Sometimes you don't know you've had it wrong until you've had it right.

Take flan, for example. The creamy custard covered in syrup used to make its way into my school lunchboxes. The little plastic cups were sold in the grocery next to snack-sized puddings and Jell-O. I loved peeling back the foil, lapping the custard off my plastic spoon and squeezing the dessert through my teeth -- which was not hard to do because I was in desperate need of braces. This, I thought to my 8-year-old self, is living. This is culture.

This is crap, I realized years later when I had my first flan that didn't come in a pack of four with a coupon for 50 cents off my next purchase. I had lived my whole 22 years of life thinking I knew what delectable dessert heaven tasted like. I was a fool! But, I ask you, how could I have known? How could I have known it was wrong when I had yet to have it right?

Yeah, yeah, OK, having to peel back the foil lid should've been an indicator that perhaps there were better options out there. But isn't that always the way of it?

We ignore the signs that say something better and more promising is possible because we have yet to experience it firsthand. Like how jeans with buttons seem great until you experience your first elastic waistband. Then, like magic, the clouds part, and angels sing. But how would you have known? You had never experienced anything better than button-down jeans. Like gummy bears before you tried the substantially better *sour* gummy bears. The carousel before your first roller coaster. Or that first boyfriend who would high-five himself every time he unhooked your bra. Or the pet goldfish before you got a dog. Or how in my teen years, I followed around the band Good Charlotte because apparently, I had yet to hear any other music. Ever.

In our ignorance, we think these things are good, but we are wrong -- so very wrong.

I just had another one of these experiences, in the form of an epidural.

My son is now 3 years old. When I was in labor with him, I experienced the worst pain I've ever had in my life. I used every trick I knew, from breathing techniques to visualization meditation to squeezing the color out of my husband's hand, but ultimately, I was still left thrashing on the bed, writing in pain. And I'd had an epidural.

Less than an hour before it was time to push, the nurses noticed I had somehow pulled the epidural drip out of my back and therefore was not receiving the medicine. They hooked me back up, and when it came time to push, though I was still able to move my legs and use my muscles to push off the stirrups, I was drugged enough for the pain to be manageable. For three years, I thought I'd had the quintessential epidural experience. Sure, there was a little hiccup, but when push came to no-seriously-it's-time-to-push, I had the same reduced pain every other laboring woman with a huge needle in her back has had.

For three years, I spread the word like gospel of the beautiful and momentarily life-altering effect of the epidural. Get the drug, I would tell new moms-to-be as if I knew what I was talking about.

How could I know I had it wrong when I had yet to have it right?

My husband and I both knew at the exact same moment that my very recent labor and delivery would be different from the first when I looked at him, glassy-eyed and smiling, and said, "I feel like a mermaid!"

That is to say, I felt nothing below my chest. I had no idea my legs had fallen off the bed until gravity began pulling the rest of my body down with them. When a doctor bent my knee up to my chest, I looked over expecting someone to be in bed with me before realizing the leg was mine. And when it came time, my daughter popped on out after three pushes to the rhythm of "If You're Happy and You Know It." It was a beautiful experience.

I thought the epidural I'd had the first time was good, but turns out it was little more than snack-sized flan in a plastic cup.

Death Glare

My daughter looks nothing like me. She doesn't look like my husband, either. I tell him it's because she looks like our mailman. Or maybe she looks more like our pizza delivery guy. My husband rolls his eyes. Then we both return to looking at our baby girl, inspecting her face, trying to find traces of ourselves in her features.

As the days following her birth passed, I began to wonder whether the child I brought home could be the result of a switched-at-birth scenario. True, she never left my side at the hospital, but still. Perhaps the baby swap wasn't unintentional. Perhaps the whole thing was orchestrated by my OB-GYN, who could have strapped a replacement baby under my hospital bed. When I gave birth, maybe she handed off my genetic mini-me to her co-conspirator nurse and placed the baby stored under the bed onto my chest. Knowing my husband would be looking anywhere other than, well, you know where, the doctor knew she'd be in the clear for this most epic of baby swaps. It all made perfect sense!

Now, sure, there was the question of why my doctor would swap out my baby for another, but answers could easily be found. For example, perhaps she had been wrong in saying I was pregnant with a girl. When she noticed I was having a son in my last ultrasound at 36 weeks, she masterminded this switched-at-birth plan so she didn't have to admit her error. Or maybe in that same 36-week ultrasound, she noticed I was pregnant with some kind of half human, half beaked serpent hedgehog -- you know, the kind of offspring begotten from a mythological god's extramarital affair with a humanoid. I'm fairly certain Zeus and his siblings had scores of these half-breeds hanging around Earth a few millenniums ago. My OB-GYN, a sworn protector of the gods' secrets, swapped out Spike, my gargoyle-ish child, for a full-human baby. I, of course, don't remember this supernatural romp with a Zeus cousin, because my doctor used one of those "Men in Black" memory-erasing pens on me. With substantiated conclusions such as these, it became perfectly evident that my new baby wasn't actually my baby. Something had to be done!

But then, as the days turned to weeks and the pictures I posted on Facebook increased, the strangest thing happened. Friends began commenting on how much my daughter resembled me. What were they talking about? I didn't see it. I wanted to see it. But I just didn't. I asked my best friend what features she thought my baby girl and I shared.

"She has your facial expressions!" my friend said.

Oh. Well, that was true enough. Practically from the moment they placed her on my chest, my daughter had nailed down my scowl. When my husband held her for the first time, he said, "There's the contemptuous, judgmental death glare I see from your mommy all the time."

My nearly 3-week-old daughter looks at everyone with disdain and utter embarrassment -- which has made me realize two things. 1) We are completely screwed when she becomes a teenager. And 2) if this is the facial expression associated with looking like me, I really ought to take some kind of acting class to mask my feelings better -- or just begin wearing masks. Yeah, that'll probably be easier.

Hey, it's not my fault. Shakira's hips don't lie, and neither do my eyebrows.

I told my friend that my daughter still may have been switched at birth, because I believe mimicking expressions has to do with nurture, not nature.

"Are you giving your new daughter your contemptuous, judgmental death glares?" she asked.

No. No, I wasn't. And why does everyone have the same name for my signature scowl?!

"So how can it be nurture if she hasn't seen it? It's in her genes."

I don't know whether I agree, but whether it's taught or inherited, I'm fairly certain the shared look marks my first parenting mistake with my daughter.

That being said, once everyone remarked on this mother-daughter resemblance, I began connecting with my girl a bit more. And as the days went on and her newborn puffiness settled, I could see she has my chin. And my husband's freaky toes. Maybe she is mine. All mine.

And if you say otherwise, my daughter and I will stare you down.

~ ~ ~

Chapter 7

"I Know You Can Wander. And I Know You Can Lust. But Can You Ever Just Lust Wander?"

"I Think You Can in Europe": Travels

World Cup at the White Castle

When I was 19 years old, I lived in Australia in a house with six other expatriates -- three Americans, two Germans and a Bulgarian. We lovingly referred to our home as the White Castle. For one, the white boxy house stood at the very top of a huge hill and could be seen from far and wide. And secondly, it was the most disgusting cesspool of filth and vermin that any human being has ever had the displeasure of living in. It was ground zero for the birth of the bubonic plague, the death of the dinosaurs and the weird radioactive green ooze that resulted in the Teenage Mutant Ninja Turtles. I'm sure of it.

Situated in the middle of a paved-over rain forest, the castle had no heating, air conditioning, fans or screens. We were forced to leave the windows open to prevent death by heat exhaustion, and each night, the ceiling would turn black from the bugs that flew in. Each morning, we would sweep up the bugs that now carpeted the floor as armies of ants tore apart the dying insects. Huntsman spiders the size of our hands lived in our bathroom. Poisonous redback spiders hung out under the toilet seat. Every morning, I would shake out my clothes so the cockroaches could fall out before I got dressed. For a few weeks, I was convinced I had contracted herpes when bumps started appearing in my nether region, only to discover that bedbugs had shacked up in the teddy bear that I cuddled nightly.

Six- and eight-legged friends weren't the only creepy-crawlies that came into our home regularly. My roommate with the basement bedroom worked as a call girl, inviting in two-legged pests along with the rest of the vermin.

But when I think back to my time living in the White Castle, I don't think of the disgusting living conditions. I think of the World Cup.

As an American without any athletic ability, I never saw soccer as being anything more than that sport with the cool ball that I would trip over between Gatorade breaks when I was 7. It was a game for children, a training ground for more important future activities, such as Hacky Sack. I had heard of the World Cup but didn't really know what it was. It never once had occurred to me that I could watch soccer on television. And really, why would I?

The White Castle changed all that.

Soon after we all moved in, the games began. As ours was one of the few houses furnished with a television, neighbors from Italy, the Netherlands, Sweden and, of course, Australia came over to watch. The energy, the excitement, the heartache -- I had never experienced such live-and-die-by fandom. It was intoxicating. Our castle hummed well into the night, and for once, it wasn't from the moth wings.

The World Cup brought our home and neighbors together in a way that, I believe, nothing else could. It resulted in an immediate introduction to the differences and similarities in our cultures. The nations would battle it out in our common room as they simultaneously did on the field. There would be screaming, cursing, brooding, cheering, kicking over the upside-down cups that covered our floors -- each with a trapped cockroach inside, as we were attempting to kill them off one by one.

After one particularly heartbreaking missed goal, my German roommate Heinz kicked our wall. The White Castle was built so shoddily that Heinz's foot went completely through the wall and got stuck on the outside of our house. From that day forward, we didn't just have bugs flying in through open windows. We had snakes and rodents crawling in, too. But that didn't stop a crowd from forming at our castle every evening.

Enemies one night, reconciled friends the next, teaming up to cheer for or against a different country. In the thick, sticky air, you could feel the racing heartbeats. Endless rounds of cold beer provided the only buffer between the heat from outside and the heat from within. All of us together. Winning together. Losing together. Suffering together. Celebrating together.

The World Cup games became the breeding ground for friendships I still carry with me, a decade after leaving the Land

Down Under. And thanks to that hole Heinz's foot created, I'm guessing, it became the breeding ground for many other animals, as well.

The Great Pyramids

"Do not sign up if you are claustrophobic, are afraid of the dark, have back problems, have knee problems, have heart problems, have lung problems, have asthma, are pregnant, are out of shape, get migraines, are prone to fainting or currently have a weakened immune system from a cold or another ailment. Are sure you want to do this?"

I have a problem saying no.

My new husband and I were trekking around Egypt for our honeymoon and finally had gotten to the Great Pyramids of Giza. The bus driver informed us that one of the pyramids was open for tourists to walk into but that we should weigh the pros and cons. Once in, there was no turning back.

I looked at my newly declared life partner, the man who had just sworn before our friends and family that he would stand by my side through thick and thin, the man who had just stated a mere week prior that he loved me for my wild side and vowed to live out every adventure with me. He saw the eager questioning in my eyes, the silent plea for him to go down into the bowels of the pyramid with me, and said, "I'm not going down there."

As it turned out, I was the only person on our bus not deterred by the driver's warning. It's not that I wasn't nervous; I just have a condition when it comes to saying no. It's why I've had so many close calls with death. It's why my body is covered in scars. Believe me, I'm not saying I'm smart. It's a condition, I tell ya. A condition!

The line to get into the pyramid was long. Clearly, the other tourists arrived via less fatalistic bus drivers. It was the dead of summer, and I was boiling by the time I reached the opening to the 3,000-year-old structure. But I did not yet know heat. The second I stepped into the pyramid, I was body-slammed by the immense heat and stifling humidity. It was hard to breathe, and I immediately was soaked down to my underpants in sweat.

Within 10 steps, the tunnel becomes dramatically tighter. One shoulder glides against the damp pyramid wall as the other shoulder gets bashed every other second by the tourists who have made the loop and are on their way out. The ceiling is so low that you have to bend at the waist, virtually sticking your nose in the anus of the person in front of you.

I was cursing my condition, when the British tourist in front of me said to his buddy before him, "I don't feel so good, mate." His friend said, "Oh, man, I'm glad I'm not walking behind you."

But I was!

Just as I was looking for a possible exit strategy, the British man let one rip, right on my face. There was no escaping it.

Suddenly, everything became very real to me. I was walking down a long tunnel in sweltering heat toward a grave, a Pharaoh's empty tomb. Death lingered in this place. These tunnels were not meant for the living. I was breathing the same stagnant air that had been sitting, hovering, in the same location for millenniums. And now this jerk had just farted in this holy place, leaving his stench to linger in these stagnant tunnels for all time?!

The two Britons started laughing. And the man in front of me farted again.

I lost it. I screamed, "Dude! Stop farting in the Pyramids!"

Words I never imagined I'd scream. The Brits stopped laughing, and we trudged on. I saw the empty grave. It was just a slab of stone. Then I hunched back down and followed someone else, nose to anus, back out.

When I got outside, the 103-degree day felt like a cold shower. I breathed deeply. My husband asked me, "Was it worth it?"

I finally learned to say no. Something my brand-new husband was probably less than thrilled about.

With a Name Like Death Valley, What Could Go Wrong?

I love the desert. It calms me.

My husband planned a surprise weekend away to Death Valley for my birthday. Into the vast emptiness. Into the suffocating heat. With an infant. Because that's the kind of geniuses we are.

From the very beginning, it felt as if the trip was cursed. Erratic traffic almost caused a handful of accidents before we left the city limits. The gas pump at the station wouldn't work. And worse yet, the Popeyes drive-thru ran out of biscuits! If that's not a sign the world is ending, I don't know what is.

An hour into our trip, the GPS inexplicably had us exit the highway and start going back the way we came.

You'd think that when the universe clearly screams to stay away from a place called Death Valley, I would listen. I'm not very smart.

Miraculously, we arrived at our hotel in the small tourist town of Shoshone, California, at 11:30 p.m. The town -- which consists of little more than a post office, gas station, cafe and inn -- was pitch-dark. No worries. Shoshone only exists to cater to out-of-towners like me. I wasn't concerned.

I should've been concerned. I knocked on the office door. Nothing. I tried to call the hotel number. No cell service. I tried using OnStar. Forget what the commercials say; the OnStar didn't have service, either.

I still wasn't too nervous when a patron of the hotel approached and said the office had closed at 10 o'clock. No one would be back until morning. He pointed me in the direction of the nearest town, 30 miles away.

Six hours after setting off on our trip, we found ourselves driving down a dark road, past midnight, looking for open motels. Every place was closed or booked. Even the super-skeezy casino inns were closed. What casino closes at midnight? Don't they rely on the poor choices of the exhausted and inebriated?

By this point, my baby had enough and was in hysterics in the back seat. I was near hysterics in the front seat. We contemplated sleeping in the car but thought Child Protective Services might look down on that. We kept driving. At some point, OnStar service began working again. They booked us at the closest hotel that was open -- another 40 miles away.

When we arrived (after getting lost because we were given the wrong hotel name), we were greeted by a black cat. The owner said his name was Spooky. It felt fitting.

It was nearly 2 a.m. The heater only blew frigid air. The lights were broken.

Our hotel once housed military personnel working at Area 51. I wondered whether aliens were punking me. I truly hoped the Ashton Kutcher of Mars would jump out with a sideways trucker hat and video camera.

Have you encountered minor inconveniences that wouldn't normally register but, when you're already irritable, seem huge? I

105

hear you and raise you my morning: I lost my contact in my eye and had left my deodorant at home, and the continental breakfast was Little Debbie cakes and a coffee pot that looked full but was actually just stained, and the only maps to Death Valley were in Spanish, and the carpet left a film on our feet, marking the first time I bathed my child in Purell. Mm, alcohol-y clean.

When my husband left to get gas, I was walked in on while breast-feeding and then promptly kicked out of my room, left to wait in the cold with my baby.

Pacing outside the front office, I overheard two hotel workers chatting.

"Room 14's complainin'. Same ol', same ol'. AC don't turn off. Lights don't turn on. Window's broken."

"Guess I'll get tinkerin' then," said the second worker.

"Best turn off the 'lectricity 'fore ya tinker."

"Don't worry," the worker said. "I tweren't really gonna tinker."

We grabbed breakfast in a smoke-filled casino, where I was served bacon inside my vegetarian omelet because, apparently, pigs don't count as animals.

At long last, we made it inside Death Valley National Park, where we were greeted by a broken pay machine. I panicked we'd be arrested by park police. The jails in Death Valley can't be comfy.

But driving around that breathtakingly beautiful basin, the desert began doing its job. It calmed me. Heaven knows how. Maybe it was the bacon.

Hating Seasickness

I write this -- with difficulty.

My head, at long last, is above my knees. A white plastic-lined paper bag is propped open on the table beside me, waiting for anything that may ... come up.

They say that when you are suffering from seasickness, at first you are afraid you are going to die. Then you are afraid you never will.

What the collective "they" fail to mention is the insurmountable desire to take everyone down with you.

I write this sitting on the lido deck of a cruise ship sailing toward the British Virgin Islands. Not on one of the long lounge chairs you could curl up in the fetal position and sleep away your seasickness on. No, those were snatched up by folks with cast-iron stomachs who rose with the sun and secured spots with towels, thus claiming the most desired location and lounge chairs for their friends and family. Friends and family who have yet to show their faces.

Dear people who snatched the lounge chairs but haven't used them:

Don't worry; it's cool. I'm dying over here, but I'll just pull up another straight chair to awkwardly spread my body across. Never mind the backache that this will cause or the weird tweak in my neck. The important thing is that you will be comfortable, should you ever choose to appear. And don't worry about snatching up all the spots in the sun. Seeing as I haven't forfeited all of MY towels staking claim to territory I will never settle in, I have plenty of blue terrycloth to wrap around my shoulders and legs to hide my unshakeable trembling from the incessant vomiting. Thank you for your concern, though.

Perhaps you comfort criminals will eventually notice my dire state and will offer me one of your untouched lounge sanctuaries warming in the Caribbean sun. Of course, to notice me, you would first have to leave the 24-hour buffet. What a pity to miss out on your fourth helping of chicken tikka masala, beef Wellington and sashimi. I've heard it's good. I've eaten pretty well myself. So far, I've managed to keep down some pretty fine dinner rolls and half a plain baked potato.

Yours hatefully,

Katiedid

It's not all the lounge chair lifters' fault; they are far from the only people worth hating while I sit here stewing in my own misery. Oh, no, there are so many hate options. Options everywhere! People doing the limbo! People in the belly flop competition! Every person cha-chaing in the conga line! High on today's hate list are ice cream eaters -- one lactose lover, in particular.

Before I mustered the energy to pry myself from my rocking bed (not the good kind) and threw on some mismatched attire (I use the term "threw," but the process was painstakingly slow) to exit my dark bedroom of death and wish for my early demise in a sunnier locale, healthier folks made their own way up to the lido deck and plopped their bottoms down in nearly every seat not occupied by the dry towels of the lounge chair leeches. I don't fault these healthy cruisers. They have a right to their calypso music, pina coladas, floral button-up shirts and embarrassing attempts at line dancing. But their leaving only the spots near the ice cream machine vacated for the late-to-rise sick and weary like me was truly cruel.

Not only am I sick but now people in a constant line are bumping into my side-by-side chairs, taking little to no notice of my barf bag or the incredible triumph of my head resting above my waist. They mock me with their smiling faces, sea legs and chocolate-vanilla swirl.

Misery loves company, and I was debating which of these cone connoisseurs I wished my queasy constitution on the most, when a man I had seen twice before waiting in line for soft-serve suddenly doubled over and announced aloud, "I think I'm gonna hurl." In that moment, I did not let him experience the embarrassment I had of vomiting on the floor of this fine ship. No, I decided to be a bigger person. I handed him my barf bag.

He held it before him, readying for the eruption. Then ... he sneezed.

He handed the bag back to me, saying, "False alarm. Good maternal instincts, though."

Dear Sneezy Guy: Go bless yourself.

Vacation With a Baby

I am on day four of a weeklong beach vacation. Many warned that vacationing with a 9-month-old is no vacation at all. But to those ninny-pooper naysayers, I have one thing to say: Pish-posh. I completely disagree. Like a college frat boy watching the clock strike 12:01 a.m. on his 21st birthday, a baby holds the true meaning of this sacred time close to his heart.

In my humble opinion, any good vacation can be quantified in how well you slept, ate and played. Luckily, my 9-month-old believes in the same mathematical formula. However, the outcome of the equation varies greatly from my own. When it comes to vacationing with a pre-walking, pre-talking pre-toddler, I have a lot to learn.

--Sleep.

The old me would say that a good vacation provides ample

108

opportunity to sleep in, to nap, to recharge. Turns out I was wrong. Sleep is for sissies.

My son has decided to fully immerse himself in this vacation. Why waste time under the covers when there is a whole world to explore? Which is why he has decided to stay up. All night. Every night.

Sure, one could argue that he is having trouble sleeping because of the new location and strange bedding. But I say poppycock! Clearly, my proactive procreation simply has a strong desire to experience the local nightlife. To club-hop and pub-crawl. To absorb the indigenous culture of the witching hours in a way that would make even traveling boozer and full-time curmudgeon Anthony Bourdain smile.

My kid's no nighttime elitist. He wants to carpe diem by daylight, too. Despite the fact that we are on vacation and can sleep past our strict weekday 6:33 a.m. wake-up time, he is insisting we all stick to it. Why sleep in?! This is vacation, for goodness' sake! What better time to wake up super-early after being up all night? Who cares that no place is open yet and that our hotel doesn't even have coffee in the lobby at that time? Isn't it just great to be awake and be alive?! My 9-month-old thinks so.

--Food.

My son is new to the world of solid foods. And I can't imagine his packaged organic mashed-up mush has really sold him on the idea. But despite being new to cuisine, my baby believes that when you are on vacation, you must try all the local fare. He must! Why else would he have insisted on putting every single seashell, perfectly sized for asphyxiation, into his mouth? You would think that somewhere on the beach, we could find a spot that lacked the veritable smorgasbord of suffocating snacks, but no.

I'm not nearly so culinarily curious or daring with dining as my son. I told him that we can learn from each other. He has inspired me to try new things, but I would prefer he develop a more dignified palate and not stick everything into his mouth. Despite being only 9 months old, my child opted to do the mature thing. He dropped the seashells and chose to eat fistfuls of sand instead.

--Play.

Before heading on our beach vacation, I bought a baby tent that blocks 99 percent of ultraviolet rays. I placed the tent next to the blanket on which I was lying and filled it with an assortment of toys. But did my son want to play in the safe harbor I had created for him? Of course not! He wanted to explore and play, dang it! He opted to let us know by exercising his lungs, as if to cry out: Life is meant to be lived, not to be idly watched as the waves of life pass you by! And what better place to trash a tent, thrash in the sand, unleash yourself from cultural expectations and sing your heart out to the beat of crashing waves? Sure, it's possible the people sleeping near us may have found my son's auditory declarations to be less inspirational and more on a par with "screaming." But I feel fairly certain the same things were said about Bjork, and she's been nominated for Grammys.

My 9-month-old understands what vacation is all about. It's about dancing in the moonlight and feeling sand under your toes and seashells in your mouth. And I can get down with that. I really can. The only problem is that I need a vacation to recuperate from this one.

A Hare-owing Tale

My dad thinks he's short.

He is 6 feet 1 inch tall.

One of four boys, all of whom grew to towering heights of 6'5" or taller, my dad is a shrimp by comparison. You know, the same way Scarlett Johansson is a disgusting old warty hag when compared with Helen of Troy. I doubt Scarlett's sent a single canoe off to war, let alone launched a thousand ships.

I've always been flabbergasted that my dad, a man who has spent most of his life looking down at people, could feel small, that his factually knowing the bulk of the population is shorter than he is could be overridden by memories of a childhood among giants. Not getting the part of Tiny Tim in his school play must've been the shock of his life.

Growing up, I mocked my dad's perception problems. I, unlike him, would surely never struggle with such a ridiculous dimension dilemma.

My driver's test would suggest otherwise.

I blame my genetic disposition for my inability to parallel park. Clearly, it is Dad's fault that I never fully grasped the largeness of my vehicle or the smallness of the space I was meant to fit into. I failed my first driver's test. But c'mon, don't most 16-year-olds fail the first time? Then I failed it again. *Thanks a lot, Dad!* And I failed again. I failed that test six times until I was able to parallel park correctly and overcome the paternal genes that were hindering me from hitting the road. My first driver's license picture sports an expression of relief more than excitement. And I'm sure it's purely coincidence that so many folks commented on how much I looked like my father in that photo.

The driving drama was far from ideal, but for as much as I blamed my dad for my parking problems -- as any teen engaging in the proper amount of angst would -- I felt confident my spatial issues remained far from his height dysmorphia. I understood that my car was big. It's not as if I thought it was really small and that's why I couldn't park. Unlike Dad, I wasn't confused; I was just inept.

Last weekend, my little family of three headed out into the wild to decompress in nature. As a parent, hiking creates contradictory concerns. I want my son to feel confident on his own two feet. I want him to run and jump and explore. But because we stay off trails, I also don't want those adorable two feet to enjoy the pleasure of an adorable two-fanged snakebite. I'm constantly in flux, deciding to let him run free, regretting my decision and picking him up, only to set him down to run free again. Recently, my mode of operation has been to hold his hand and teach my survival training as we stroll. I point out prickly bushes, poisonous leaves and perfect hiding spots for creepy-crawlies. Certainly, at 24 months, he commits everything I say to long-term memory.

My son is currently obsessed with animals. We have an 18-pound rabbit at home, who is his best friend and often preferred to parents. On the last day of our outing, I told my son we would look for rabbits on our hike.

Jumping around the rocks, with me pointing out potential dangers, it wasn't long before we saw a hare in the distance. I scooped up my son and began to run toward it. It was fast and scampered away, only leaving its tall, pointed ears for me to track its movement by. After a five-minute pursuit, the hare had run down an embankment. Confident we'd be close to the fluffy friend when we hit the top of the hill we were climbing, I considered putting my son down, but I hesitated.

Thank goodness.

Two steps later and we were only about 30 feet from the hare we were chasing. But it wasn't a hare; it was a coyote. And now instead of running, it was staring back at us.

Despite knowing that hares are relatively small, I must have had my perception altered by living with an 18-pound relative for the past four years. When I saw a big brown fluffy creature in the distance with pointy ears, what else could it have been but a lagomorph like mine?

"Coyote," I said to my son as I backed away cautiously. "No touch."

My son said, "Cyo. No touch." Everything's a teaching opportunity. *Thanks, Dad.*

Summer Blues for Vegetarians

I am a terrible vegetarian.

For starters, I eat meat. Well, fish. But I tell myself the honey-glazed salmon and sesame-crusted sashimi on my plate are really just Pepperidge Farm Goldfish. It alleviates the guilt of not actually being a true vegetarian but rather being a pescetarian. And let me tell you, living as a pescetarian gets you zero points from both vegetarians and full-fledged bacon-lovin' omnivores alike.

Apparently, my diet is a deep offense in its own right, as my friend and fellow Piscean often points out, calling me cannibalistic for eating the animal of my astrological sign. I am not only a vegetarian who eats meat but also a vegetarian who cannibalizes.

Sadly, being born a day later, under the Aries sign, wouldn't have solved all my problems. I wear my faux-vegetarianism like a medal around my neck, literally. More than 10 years ago, I took a hunk of bone into my hand and carved it into a fishhook necklace, which I have never taken off. It's a daily reminder that despite my giving up most meat when I was 14 years old, I'm not exactly spokeswoman material.

But that's not even the worst part. What makes me a terrible vegetarian isn't the fact that I still eat animals. What makes me a terrible vegetarian isn't the fact that I wear a huge hunk of bone around my neck, Pebbles Flintstone-style. What makes me a terrible vegetarian is that I still miss meat. And no time of year makes me question my convictions like summertime.

It is an impossibility that any sane person ever chose to curb meat consumption during the summer. How could anyone? The campfire culinary concoctions! The grilling! The barbecues! The sweet smell of smoked hide that fills the neighborhood. The fast-food pit stops en route to the beach! The corn dogs at the amusement park! The giant turkey leg at the Renaissance fair! No, is that one just me? OK, fine, the deep-fried chicken and Krispy Kreme doughnut sandwiches at the county fair! C'mon, I know I can't be the only vegetarian who salivates over those crazy cardiac arrest cakes!

This summer has proved to be especially difficult for me, for one main reason: emus.

Yes, emus.

During a shining streak of something special, another lifetime and many moons ago, I worked as an adventure tour guide in the Outback. There, I befriended an aboriginal shaman who opened up his land for our adventures. During one of those weeks, the metallic strands in my hair scrunchie caught the eye of an emu, leading to five of the most terrifying minutes of my life.

My shaman grabbed a piece of wood and chased away my giant winged nemesis. He returned more than an hour later, dragging the dead bird behind him.

He dropped the emu by my feet and said, "Dinner."

That day, my diet adopted an addendum: If you attack me, I will eat you!

The emu was cooked into a stew over an open fire in the wild of the Outback. And it was the most delicious thing I have ever eaten. Scaring the living daylights out of someone can really amp up an appetite!

I scarfed down the stew, knowing full well that my body no longer knew how to metabolize meats. Knowing full well that I would probably become ill and would suffer greatly for this act of gourmet revenge. But I didn't care. And, miraculously, I didn't get sick. It's as if my stomach signed on to the new "attack clause" in my diet.

The emu incident never made me second-guess my diet. I went back to being the same terrible vegetarian I always was. Everything returned to status quo. Until this summer.

My in-laws came to visit and took us to an emu farm, where we could feed the birds. It was supposed to be a gift for my animal-loving son, but the winged wackos were so aggressive I couldn't let my toddler near the fence. The emu farm did not provide the family-friendly adventure we had anticipated, but it did effectively remind me of my intense hatred of emus. And in turn, it reminded me how delicious emus are.

Last night, I smelled an exquisite aroma coming from my neighbors' backyard as they were grilling dinner. They had picked up emu patties from a shop down the street.

I may not be a pescetarian by summer's end.

Toddlers in Tents

Last weekend, my group of friends and I headed off to our annual camping trip. Over the years, we have solidified this event -- the number of people invited, the location, the food, the sun-to-beer-to-hangover ratio.

We've learned and adapted from mistakes of the past. A ghost sighting from two years prior resulted in our positioning the tent door so it faced a different direction. Last year's windstorm resulted in splintered poles and the purchase of a new tent altogether. We've had footballs impaled on Joshua trees. We've had our football throwing arms impaled on Joshua trees. And we've experienced that terrifying feeling in your gut of being truly lost in the wilderness more than once. But this year, we encountered a new camping challenge -- a force stronger than a windstorm, scarier than a ghost. This year, our camping trip included a toddler.

Camping has always been my form of meditation, my yoga. It's how I unwind. Turns out that it's hard to feel serene with your toddler teetering on the edge of a cliff while you scream, "Stop trying to kill yourself while Mommy is trying to harness her Zen!"

I'm fairly confident I just quoted the Buddha.

 sweaty chasing my son around the rocky terrain, steering him away from snake holes, bees and sunburn. Suddenly, it's clear why all my children died from snakebites every time I played "Oregon Trail." The whole family could have made it out West if, instead of exploring, the youngest digital settlers would have stayed in their wagon, playing Nintendo DS and singing songs from "Frozen" as their mother wanted.

I'm guessing that's pretty historically accurate.

My son broke my camping calm with his dirt-digging, valley-screaming, rock-climbing antics, but after a while, I decided to stop fighting it. This trip wouldn't be about tents and tranquility. This trip was meant to be about experiencing the great outdoors through the eyes of a toddler. And once I allowed myself to stop running after my son and instead run with him, I could see his little mind figuring out how the whole wilderness thing works. I could practically hear his inner monologue as he discovered all the wonderful things about camping that I take for granted. It laced even the grossest parts of the weekend with a little bit of magic.

Below are 10 things my son learned about camping, said in the voice I imagine his inner monologue to sound like:

1) Outhouses are amazing. They provide awesome echoes after your screams and have a super-cool hole you can climb down into. For some weird reason, my mama kept chasing after me every time I sneaked away to the outhouse, waving her arms, and stopped me before I could go spelunking -- this time.

2) Why sit on an anthill when you can sit on a red anthill? Just saying, we're in the woods; let's live dangerously.

3) Nature is best explored naked.

4) Hammocks are so much fun but are impossible to get out of. You don't think my folks knew that when they put me in the hammock ... and then kept putting me in. They wouldn't do that to me, right? Nah.

5) Food tastes better with mud on your hands. Even better with crushed bugs between your fingers. Try to bite me again, red ant. Just try it.

6) Chili causes some serious diaper rash. For reals, y'all. I couldn't sit or stand for a full 24 hours after that blasted bean-fest. What is chili pepper made of, pure fire?

7) Speaking of fire, the campfire calls to me. It whispers, "Touch me. Jump in me. Don't be afraid of the heat. I'll give you a warm hug."

8) Moms cannot hear the siren call of campfires. They pull you away every time you try to jump in. Moms are terrible campers.

9) Tents are so much fun to run around in but impossible to unzip. Do you think my folks knew that when they zipped up the door? They wouldn't do that to me, right? Nah.

10) If your lame parents hinder you from injuring yourself while camping, slam your fingers in the car door on your way home. Can't leave a trip without a battle wound.

...Are the Luckiest People

It's not you; it's me. I just don't really like ... people.

It's not because of some shy, reactive response to being surrounded by people. Nor do people fill me with rage in a Lewis Blackian maelstrom of spat expletives, shaking hands and throbbing forehead veins that will result in an inevitable early demise via cardiac arrest. (In case I miss the moment it actually happens, here's a pre-emptive "R.I.P., Lewis Black." I love ya, you rabid little goofball.) I don't like people because of our sheer quantity. So when I won a free trip to anywhere in the continental United States from Skyscanner, my first and foremost concern was getting far away from people.

No offense.

Skyscanner is one of those awesome websites that I, a semi-retired travel junkie, am always looking at to facilitate fantasies of destinations farther away than where my son goes for day care. I love websites such as Skyscanner. I love plugging in different destinations and comparing costs of buying a plane ticket, booking a hotel and renting a car. I take a screenshot of the final price and itinerary and store it away in a desktop folder titled "Future."

My Skyscanner giveaway win, in some way, felt predetermined. As if one of the prankster Dreamtime creatures I had learned about when studying under an Aborigine in the Outback had been peering over my shoulder at the pathetically ever-expanding desktop folder of future adventures and taken immense pity on me. I like to think the little troll sneaked into Skyscanner's offices and blew up all the computers that had documented the original contest winner's name, used some crazy ninja voodoo trick to erase the memory of the employees and then fogged up the bathroom windows and wrote, "Katiedid wins. Or else." But that's probably not exactly how it went down. Obviously. I mean, where would those little mystical creatures have learned to spell?

After taking an obnoxiously long time to decide on a vacation itinerary, undoubtedly testing the unwavering patience and kindness of the Skyscanner team, I held the airplane tickets to Portland, Oregon, in my hands. A five-day road trip into the peace, quiet and solitude of rural Beaver State areas. Far away from people.

Day one was spent hiking to and from waterfalls. They were exquisite and lush, and I had forgotten how fresh it is to breathe in the scent of moss-covered branches and stones. Huffing dried oregano in preparation for the trip was not the same. And it may have stung a little.

That night, not only were we the only guests at an amazing cabin retreat but also when the owners learned it was my birthday, they planned an incredible breakfast of blueberry creme brulee French toast and booked a massage for me to have out on the patio, overlooking the mountains and my giggling toddler chasing butterflies in the high grasses.

Then we headed inland, passing through 10-building towns sparsely populated with kind folk who made sure to tell us which town to eat in and where to get gas -- one time informing us that the next opportunity would be three towns away and at least a 70-mile drive.

We stayed one night at a historical house near the Painted Hills that rents out its rooms as a hotel. Locals spent the evening in the hotel's living room, playing cards, playing piano and watching television, merry and obliging to the dumbfounded tourists who struggled with the lack of cell service and Internet access.

We dined at a cafe where a woman drove in to pick up pie but realized she had forgotten which slice her husband wanted. She was about to drive the 30 miles back home to get his order, when the cafe owner said, "You can call him if you want." The local looked in awe, "You got a phone here?"

"Sure do. Going on eight months now." I smiled at the cafe owner, and she beamed back at me.

During the whole trip, we were given kind smiles and unsolicited travel tips, and keen interest in our origins and destinations was shown. The trip ended with our spending a day in Portland with a college pal whom I hadn't seen in eight years, and I boarded the plane back home thrilled by how easy it had been to fall back in step with my old friend.

I went to Oregon to get away from people, but it was the people who made the trip.

Destination Wedding

I hate to fly. Since having my son, I've tried to do it as little as possible. It's one thing to send myself 30,000 feet into the sky without a parachute or flying squirrel suit, but I'm fairly confident endangering my innocent toddler warrants a visit from Child Protective Services.

This summer, my husband, toddler and big ol' belly housing a half-baked fetus will be taking to the oh-dear-Lord-let-them-be-friendly skies. Then we take to them again. And again. One of my dear friends is getting married on a tiny German island off the coast of Denmark. To say traveling there is easy is to be a big fat liar. Like, a liar on a sociopathic level. Like, your pants are so on fire it's as if you never even had pants in the first place.

Sylvie and I met in another world, in another time that often feels like a million years ago. In reality, that other world was Australia, and those million years were just over a decade. She was my first flatmate after I moved across the globe for a year of adventure and self-discovery, in a disgusting, dilapidated, bug-infested house we lovingly named the White Castle. There is a special bond that grows between roommates when you live in such peril, every morning being greeted by the large fangs of the huntsman spider living in our shower, every evening having our bodies eaten alive by the creatures that swarmed through our screenless windows into our air conditioning-less house situated in the middle of a rain forest. We were in the trenches together. The filth, grime and impenetrable heat and humidity together. To say we are familiar with each other's body odor is like saying you've heard of that Meryl Streep person. She's an actress, right?

Over the years, we've stayed in touch, managing to see each other every few years. We saw each other through new relationships. New homes. New jobs. New babies. Her fiance introduced me to every spiced wine in the Christmas markets when I was unaware I was two weeks pregnant and insists the wine is what has made my son so sweet.

When someone whom you share such a history with decides to get married on a tiny island across land and ocean, you do what any person with a fear of flying would do. You make a mediocre attempt to look for a flight and set a price point so low it seems unachievable. Curse you, CheapOair and your low prices!

118

We fly first to Boston. Then we'll push our toddler-tantrum luck by boarding another plane from there to Iceland. All I know about Iceland is that USA played its team in the shamefully Oscar-snubbed film "D2: The Mighty Ducks" and that we have a two-day layover there. People have told me that Reykjavik is a great party town -- which is great because I'm betting that my six-month baby bulge is going to want to bounce to the bumpin' club beats until dawn. And by bouncing to the bumpin' club beats, what I really mean is sleep. After defying both the laws of gravity and the conceivable human decibel level with terrified screams on the plane, I may just sleep for our entire two-day layover. But hey, at least the view from my hotel window will be all Elsa, Anna and Olaf -- you know, before I close the blackout curtains so I can slumber.

After another five-hour flight to Hamburg, a long trek on a train and a ferry ride, we will finally arrive at the tiny island for this destination wedding. After less than a week of festivities, we will do the whole trip in reverse. John Candy and Steve Martin will have had nothing on me! Except for an awesome mustache. I'd love me a John Candy mustache.

I've been told that being six months pregnant is the best way to fly. Not only do you get to wear a sexy pair of compression pantyhose but also you get to enjoy frequent trips to the bathroom. But even with all this competition, I'm betting that the best part of the trip will be watching my beautiful friend marry the man she loves. And if I toast her with one sip of German wine to ensure my current bun in the oven turns out as sweet as my first one, so be it. Cheers.

Vacation

There were many things we knew we had to prepare for prior to taking six planes, four trains and two buses to attend my friend's wedding. You don't take on a trip like that with a toddler and a grumpy pregnant lady with closed eyes. And you don't take such a crazy trip unless it's for a very good friend. (Un)fortunately, this was for a very good friend -- a friend who stood by my side as we battled poisonous spiders, venomous snakes and toxic breakups. We shared three homebrewing kits, two broken fans, one prostitute roommate who used our flat in the Australian rain forest as a brothel, and half a

119

language. This is the sticky stuff, the thick and murky life ingredients that solidify into the concrete foundation of lasting friendship. This is the stuff that makes you pack passports, a toddler leash, compression stockings and a suitcase large enough to comfortably fit three bodies and a Shetland pony and voyage across a continent and an ocean.

The cheapest airfare to her wedding destination of the tiny German island off the coast of Denmark where she was raised came via Iceland. Three days were to be spent both at the top and bottom of our wedding expedition in the cold and tiny country my son referred to as Anna and Elsa's home. Accommodating a two-week trip for three people adventuring into both freezing glaciers and warm summer beaches and into a grubby subway and a fancy wedding should have had even my behemoth suitcase brimming with bathing suits, mittens and cummerbunds. But it wasn't. No, my suitcase was in danger of bursting zippers and exceeding weight limitations because of a surplus of coloring books and action figures.

I'm not a big fan of stuff. I'm the person who sees a pile of junk and simply gets rid of it, only to realize too late I just donated my Social Security card and birth certificate to child brides in Malawi. (Come to think of it, that may have worked out for the best.) But when you're about to take on 30 hours of flying round trip with a toddler, stuff is the only way to go. We are not an iPad family, so we headed to the next best option. The dollar store.

I take my dollar stores very seriously. One is not like the other, and a good one is worth its weight in gold. OK, OK, it's worth its weight in copper pennies. You get the point. My son and I explored every aisle, buying toys that if lost would not result in a global warming-level ocean increase from toddler tantrum tears. Fingers crossed. Cars, crayons, dinosaurs, googly glasses, pillows, activity books, fake teeth, sippy cups, books, snacks, even swimmies. I left that store confident I had not missed a single thing to make my son's trip -- and therefore our trip -- as painless and enjoyable as possible.

I was wrong. So very wrong. There was one thing I saw at the dollar store and ignored that would have made all the difference in our trip: a pink ruffled, padded eye mask for sleeping.

I had considered the eye mask for the plane ride. My scope was so shortsighted. We didn't need it for the plane. We had toys galore to take care of travel. We needed it for after we landed.

Iceland is home to the midnight sun. We knew this. Alas, our hotel was not home to curtains or shades. We did not know this.

A perfectly behaved and content toddler does not stay that way for very long once he arrives to a bed in which he is completely unable to sleep. Because our suitcase was filled to the brim with toys, we hadn't packed towels, which could have helped block out the sun shining brightly into our room nearly 24 hours a day. My son would go, go, go until he passed out around 6 p.m. -- only to wake around 10:30 p.m. and want to play through the night until 5 a.m. We took walks around the empty streets of the city just as the hottest Reykjavik clubs were closing.

How, I wondered, how do people around here have children and survive? And then I realized the residents have blinds. And curtains. And possibly frilly pink padded eye masks. We may have gone into this trip with our eyes open, but it sure would've been nice to be able to close them.

~ ~ ~

Chapter 8

"You Ain't Cool Unless You Pee Your Pants": Potty Humor

A Bursting Bladder

Say what you want about Sigmund Freud, but he got one thing right: I have penis envy.

That's not to say I have penis envy in all facets of my life, but when it comes to the convenience of getting to use the world as your toilet, boys have it made. And I think most ladies would agree; it seems pretty cool to write your name in the snow.

Being a rather outdoorsy person, this potty problem has plagued me my whole life. As a child, I tried to use my resourcefulness to solve the issue. For example, whenever we went to the beach, I wouldn't build sand castles like the other silly children; I'd build a sand toilet. My mom found it unsanitary to urinate in the ocean, so my sand toilets became an architectural achievement of both comfort, relief and functionality. First, I would dig a deep hole for my feet to go in. Once I was able to sit up perfectly straight, with my feet dangling in the hole, I began work on a secondary hole about six inches back. You can guess what this one was for. But what really made my sand toilets the Taj Mahal of sand structures was the attention to detail on the seat portion and the comfortable yet strong backrest. I would sit on my sand throne like a queen, and I didn't have to move a muscle when it came time to relieve all the apple juice I'd been drinking. (Gotta stay hydrated when building a sand toilet.)

When I was older, I spent a lot of time camping. It was during this time I perfected the tree-hugger, the spot-and-squat, the potato leak, the rock-and-rollaway, the Pee-Wee-Wee Herman and the Abraham Leak-oln.

If I'm being completely honest, I started to think of myself as an outdoor bathroom aficionado. But any great artist must someday face a challenge so great that it will either best him or come darn close.

My moment came when I was hiking the Inca Trail to Machu Picchu in Peru.

It was the first day of the hike and had been raining all day, and we hadn't passed a single bathroom stop. Apparently, the Incas can build a massive hidden empire, but a port-a-potty stumped them. To make matters worse, the group hiked together at one pace, and there was no opportunity to break away.

When we got to the campsite, my bladder was at risk of spontaneous combustion. I grabbed my headlamp and headed into the woods.

The bulk of the trees around our campground were either covered in thorny vines or poisonous vines. In the pitch dark and pouring rain, with nothing but my tiny headlamp, finding a place to go was becoming impossible. What I would've given for a sand toilet.

Finally, I found a tree with an exposed trunk that was surrounded by bushes. Perfect for hiding my exposed trunk. I got into position, and just as I was about to relieve myself, I heard:

Grrrrrrrrr!

I clenched. I looked from side to side, my tiny headlamp shining into the rustling bushes, but I couldn't see anything. My heart raced. Maybe I'm just losing it -- delirious from full-bladder syndrome. I began to relieve myself, when suddenly the growling got louder and the shaking of the bushes more severe. Clench!

Again, I moved my headlamp from side to side, trying to see something -- anything! -- in the dense bush, but in the darkness and rain, it was amazing I had even found this tree. I really needed to empty my bladder, but there were pumas in these parts! Was going to the bathroom really worth being torn to bits by a large-toothed mammal? But at that point, I had no control. I tried to go for the third time.

GRRRRROWWLLL!!!

Nope! Nope, nope, nope. I pulled up my pants and got back to my tent as fast as humanly possible. There would be no relief tonight.

That night, all of our tents flooded severely. We woke up drenched to the bone. And though I'd like nothing more than to blame my wet clothing on the flood, I can't ignore the fact that by sunrise, my urge to urinate was gone.

Diaper Duty

Warning: Finish your breakfast before reading this column. Seriously.

Diaper duty, schmiaper duty.

I went into parenting fearless of anything that might be emitted from my son. No matter the orifice projected from, the color or the size and whether it be liquid, solid or somewhere in between, I had it covered. Months before my due date, I had every kind of diaper rash cream stored in alphabetical order, burp cloths organized by color and wipes up the wazoo.

"You don't understand," my friends would tell me. "They puke and pee and poop. In the beginning, it's like tar. You've never seen anything like it."

"It's cool," I reassured them. "I'll visit the La Brea Tar Pits before I give birth so I know what I'm dealing with."

"This is no joke," my friends insisted. "You have no idea what it's like to be covered in that stuff."

My friends don't know me very well. I know exactly what it's like.

My preparedness for the grosser side of parenting is not only because of my obsessive-compulsive organizing of baby products but more so because of my gag reflex of steel -- a gag reflex I hardened over years of unfortunate miscommunication.

I warned you to put down that morning bagel, right?

I grew up outside Washington, D.C. Every winter, you were practically guaranteed a handful of days off school because of snow, with the perfect amount of powder to keep you sledding all day. With parents often stuck having to go to work, many of us kids were left without supervision on these most coveted of days. Our young minds focused on the only thing that mattered on snow days: Where is the biggest hill?

The best sledding hill in my neighborhood was forbidden. None of our parents, including mine, explained why we weren't allowed to sled at this most awesome of awesome hills; it was just off-limits.

With the lack of supervision that accompanied snow days, the neighborhood kids and I ignored our parents' wishes and headed over to the super sledding hill. You have to understand the allure of the sledding perfection. The hill was actually more of a crater that a ton of kids could sled down at once into the valley below. At the base of the crater was about a foot of water that would freeze over, enabling us to zip across the ice. It was sublime! Sure, the ice would break, soaking us, but we didn't care. We kept at it, assuming our parents didn't want us sledding at super hill because of the drowning risk.

Turns out they weren't afraid we would drown.

Years later, I learned the valley we'd sled into was a sewage dump. I thought I was getting covered in mud when the ice would break. I was wrong.

What's worse, I did not get wiser with age.

The summer after graduating college, I went to Israel. I'd heard a lot about the Dead Sea mud's nourishing benefits, so as I floated on the water, I pulled at the seafloor. This task proved harder than expected from the salt rocks hardening the mud. Eventually, my friend found an area where the mud was easily handled. We coated our bodies and lay out in the summer sun to let the mud harden on our skin. Sure, it smelled a little -- OK, it smelled a lot -- but what did I know? I've never been slathered in mud before. A few other friends came over to us and asked where we had found easily accessible mud. They, too, were having trouble pulling up the hardened seafloor. We pointed to where the soft mud was.

"You mean right where the sewer pipe empties out into the sea?"

Oh, gross! How we managed not to notice the sewer pipe, I will never know.

So no, I was not afraid of diaper duty or of any element that might come at me from my baby. I figured I had experienced much worse from my own stupidity. The baby was off the hook. And I was doing well. The tarlike meconium came and went. I survived the daily golden shower. I was feeling pretty darn confident that there was nothing coming out of my baby's body that would do me in or get my steel-like gag reflex going.

Last night, my son projectile vomited into my mouth.

I have so much to learn.

Potty Training

Potty training your toddler while pregnant presents an odd paradox. How can I convince him that briefs are best when all I can think about is how magical it would be to wear a diaper? Seriously, that crazy astronaut lady from a few years ago was onto something. I try not to be a hypocrite in raising my child. I actively avoid the "do as I say, not as I do" mentality. But my maternal conviction may have met its match. Prenatal Pull-Ups sound like perfection.

I believe that my toddler knows when it is time to use the potty but opts not to leave the fun activity he's engaged in. Find me a single adult person who hasn't suffered from the same dilemma. Serve your basic human functions or wait until the end of the show to see who gets the final rose or makes the final shot in the game. You can't relieve yourself now! Your fantasy relationship/football team depends on your pacing before the television set. The damage you could cause to your fellow fans -- nay, to the world!

How can I reprimand my kid when he wants to keep playing blocks or riding bikes? I get it. Potty breaks stink, and now that I'm pregnant, I don't even have to be doing something fun to want to avoid the incessant nagging of Mother Nature. Why is it that when you are running on fumes, exhausted to the core and carrying around an extra 40 pounds of weight, you are destined to hoist your heavy body off the chair/couch/elephant/random person's lap you've plopped down on and proceed to shuffle a distance that, no matter how close, seems inexorably long?

My son has expressed zero interest in potty training. I am certainly not above bribery; my son, however, is unbribable. I tried inducing him with an M&M every time he used the potty.

Nada.

I upped the ante to two M&M's. Then the whole bag. Then to toys. Hot Wheels. Action figures. I said I would give him a new puppy every time he sat on the potty. My son responded, "No, I don't think so." Which, I guess, is a blessing in disguise. If he got a puppy every time he used the potty, I'm fairly confident we'd get in trouble with a few animal rights organizations. Cruella de Vil would be put to shame with her mere 101 Dalmatians. Think of the coats we could make.

Actually, don't. That's a terrible idea.

I'm starting to think it's all a scam. While a simple sneeze, laugh or cough can give me a case of pregnancy incontinence, my son is engaged in one big bathroom ruse. And why not? It's genius. His portable training potty has been moved to a prime position in front of the television, next to all of his favorite toys. Praise, prizes and presents are plentiful. And underpants come in colorful packs with his favorite characters on them. You know how long it's been since I had my heroes on my panties? Why don't they make She-Ra underwear for adults? For the honor of Grayskull, I must find out why!

Being pregnant with my second child is a very different experience than being pregnant with my first. Replacing worry and terror is self-examination. Time is spent exploring all the things I feel I have done right in parenting so I can aim to repeat -- and exploring all the things I've done wrong so I can aim to avoid. When it comes to potty training, I think I've done a lot wrong. I can't help but think that perhaps there is another way.

My friend just got a puppy, and the pup was trained in a week. Maybe I can follow her method for my second child. We'll start on the day I take her home, just as my friend did. Sure, I'll have to line the whole house with newspaper every morning, but hey, at least I'm promoting literacy. My daughter will be at a fifth-grade reading level before she can crawl. It's hard to see a downside.

Then again...

Yesterday my son went the whole day in his new underwear without any accidents. I wish I could say the same thing. Maybe my toddler should be the one potty training me.

~ ~ ~

Chapter 9

2 School 4 Cool: Childhood

Tissue Cigarettes

When I was 13, all I wanted was to be popular. I wanted to sit with the popular kids. Eat with the popular kids. Be one of the popular kids.

So I started working on it. First on the agenda was clothing. All the cool kids were wearing jeans, so I had to have a pair. But in 1995, they didn't make jeans long enough for freakishly long limbs such as mine. The jeans ended mid-shin, and in the mid-'90s, when Nirvana reigned and grunge was in, Capri pants were not. I told my mom that I needed longer pants, but my mom told me just to pull up my socks and no one would notice. They noticed. And I was not popular.

I needed a new approach. The popular kids always had boyfriends, so in came Matthew. He had sandy blond hair, gentle lips and an amazing smile. Matt was thoughtful. Matt was smart. Matt was funny. Matt was imaginary.

I was not a savvy 13-year-old, and rather than make my imaginary boyfriend from a different school, I said he went to my school. Naturally, questions arose. Where was this Matthew? Why wasn't he in the yearbook? Did anyone have a class with this elusive sandy-haired stud who had earned the hearts I'd drawn all over my binder?

Classmates probed, and I fumbled through my lies.

"What are you talking about? I was totally holding his hand when I saw you between second period and third period."

My classmates looked at me as if I were a crazy fool, which I was, and declared, "You were alone!"

And I was not popular.

When rumors about imaginary Matthew went around school, I had to do damage control -- and fast. There was only one popular move I could think to make to combat the loserdom of a fake boyfriend: smoke cigarettes. But my parents were against smoking, as all parents should be, and I didn't want to disappoint them. That's when my best friend and fellow dork, Kate, came up with the best plan ever. We would roll up tissues to look like cigarettes and smoke those. From a distance, it would look like the real thing!

Kate and I stood close enough for kids to see us smoking but too far for them to see what we were smoking. It was perfect. Sure, we had constant burns on our fingers and lips. Tissues burn fast, ya know. But the plan was working. Instant cool status. That is, until the one day I was walking home, smoking my Kleenex, and my arch-nemesis since kindergarten sneaked up behind me.

"Hey, spot me a cig."

I didn't know what to do. I froze. The tissue burned my fingers, and I screamed out.

"What is that? Oh, my God, are you smoking a tissue?"

"No. That would be so lame."

"Oh, my God, you are smoking a tissue! You are such a freak."

I was busted.

And I was not popular.

There is only one way to combat the social suicide that comes from high-water pants with pulled-up socks, a fake boyfriend and smoking tissues:

I became a real smoker. And by the next year, I was popular.

I sat with the popular kids. I ate with the popular kids. I listened to endless vapid conversation. I laughed at jokes that weren't funny. I pretended to be interested in boring, selfish people. I lied constantly. I mocked old friends. I sneaked out of my house. I cheated. I stole.

And a few months in, I was just over it. All of it.

The following Monday, I walked past my popular friends and said, "I'm sitting somewhere else today." I approached a new group of kids, who are still my best friends today. When I asked whether I could sit with them, they said yes without hesitation. They were everything my popular friends weren't -- kind, funny, honest, interesting and smoke-free. I gave up all of my vices that day. There was no need for them here.

And again, I was not popular.

My goodness, was I not popular.

And I had the best high-school experience because of it. There is something freeing in owning your dork status. You get to do something others can't; you get to be you, high-waters and all.

Shoplifting in the Lingerie Department

"I think I found a winner," my interviewer said. "The job is yours."

I was sitting in a heavily air-conditioned office, interviewing for a job as a summer manager in a local department store. "Just give me a minute for some protocol nonsense. I have to run your name in the store database and make sure nothing scandalous pops up."

My heart skipped a beat.

The interviewer chuckled as he exited, as if finding something scandalous were some ridiculous premise that never had been substantiated. But I had a flood of memories rushing back. Padded bras. Handcuffs. Oh, no, what had I done?

Suddenly, the office looked so familiar. I had been in that very room nearly a decade prior but under very different circumstances:

"Just put it in your purse," my friend urged, handing me a bra in the middle of the department store. I looked down at my then 14-year-old body -- and then at my friend's. We were years away from needing to shop in the lingerie department. At the summer's end, we'd be entering high school as the same pancake-chested gals we were in junior high, and no amount of chanting "I must, I must, I must, I must increase my bust" was going to change that.

Sure, I had tried stuffing my training bra, but after a teacher pulled me aside to point out the red sock sticking out the top of my shirt, I figured death by embarrassment wasn't worth the risk. And there were exercises and weird blended concoctions (carrot milkshakes are oddly delicious) but none that brought on the seemingly much-needed results for the quickly approaching summer's end.

But here my friend was, holding a padded A-cup and telling me to hide it in my purse.

"This bra would make even a boy look busty. Take it."

It was my first time shoplifting.

My face flushed. I looked from side to side, wondering whether you are given orange or black-and-white striped bras in prison.

"Don't look so scared. I'm gonna try these on."

My friend walked into the changing room, wielding a handful of bras. I was alone, the evidence of my teenage corruption in my purse.

After what felt like an hour, my friend emerged sans bras.

"None of them fit?" I asked her.

"Yeah. Sure, kid. None of them fit. Let's go. And be cool."

I tried to do what my friend said. I tried to be cool. But a couple of things stood in my way: 1) I was never cool, and 2) I was shoplifting!

We made it through the first set of exit doors. No alarms went off. No flashing lights. Just five more steps to the last set of doors, when...

Bam!

We were slammed against the wall by security, handcuffed and taken to the heavily air-conditioned office for questioning.

It was my last time shoplifting.

What happened next is a blur, partly because my head was spinning, partly because everything looks blurry through a waterfall of tears.

I handed over the bra in my purse.

"And the rest of them?"

My friend tugged at her shirt. She was hiding seven bras, and I had no idea.

They called our parents, took our pictures, names and information, fined us, and said they wouldn't press charges if we swore never to step in their department store again.

We swore.

The years rolled on, and I forgot about my sordid past. I returned to shopping at the store as a paying customer. I no longer looked around for pictures with my face that read, "Have You Seen This Flat-Chested Thief?" Time had healed the wound -- so much so that when I heard the store was hiring managers, I didn't blink before printing out a resume and heading over.

And now here I was -- in the same back office, waiting for my would-be boss-to-be to return after presumably seeing my name and picture in the database of shame.

I panicked. And I did what any reasonable person would do:

I ran.

My friends, I ran like the wind. I may have broken the sound barrier. I ran, hopped in my car and never looked back.

I had sworn I never would step foot in there again, and now I meant it.

Last weekend, my neighbor gave me a gift certificate to the department store. Any takers?

Riding a Bike: It's Not for Everyone

Bicycles and I are not friends. We have a mutual understanding: If I don't get on one, one won't kill me. So when I moved across the country, I was shocked to find a bicycle in the moving truck along with my old dresser and beanbag chair. I demanded an explanation from my mom, who simply said, "One sunny day, you may wish you had one." How could it be that my own mother, my own flesh and blood, could know me so little?

I had been on a bike only twice in 15 years. Both times, I fell off, hit my head, blacked out and woke up with a broken body and a concussion.

And now here it was' again, my mortal enemy, staring me down at my very own doorstep. It had followed me across the country. It could find me anywhere. I kept the pink shiny beast chained up outside. Sometimes when I walked past, I swear the bike would call out to me: "I am your friend. Don't you think I'm pretty?" But I stayed strong. "I will not give in to you, Bicycle! You will not best me!"

Then it happened. The day my mom had forewarned.

Last week, a bright and beautiful sunny day cut through the clouds and cold that had plagued my neighborhood. Sun lovers took to the streets, moving swiftly on anything with wheels -- skateboards, scooters and bikes.

I looked over at my old foe, the two-wheeled temptress, chained up, looking sad.

And I thought, I don't want to be one of those people who live in fear, do I?

I broke the peace treaty. I unchained the bike.

Running my hands over the handlebars, I pleaded, "Please, please. No injuries. No falling. Please." And my pretty bike acquiesced to my request. I did not fall. But a true nemesis always has a trick up its sleeve. I should have known never to trust a Trojan horse, or, in my case, a Huffy.

I hit the streets of my neighborhood. I was shaky. As I slowly swerved from side to side, a line of cars formed behind me. I waved my arm, signaling for them to go around, but there wasn't enough room, and I knew that. Then the honking began. I had to take to the sidewalk, the scary sidewalk, where roots had jutted up slabs of concrete and any number of atrocities could be waiting to bring me to my knees.

Terrified, I looked around for hope, for a sign I was meant to continue on this fear-facing journey. And that's when I saw my bicycle guru.

A young boy, about 7 years old, zigzagged his way down the jagged sidewalk. This kid knew these streets. He knew how to ride, how to survive. It was magnificent. I pedaled behind him, giving him a friendly wave hello when he looked to see who was on his tail.

I mimicked the kid's movements down the streets of our neighborhood, delighting in how well I was doing. No longer having to worry about the sidewalk perils underwheel, I was able to work just on my riding. Not to brag or anything, but I was doing awesome!

The kid pedaled faster and faster, down the neighborhood streets and into a cul-de-sac. I followed, thrilled I could ride fast enough to keep up with my new buddy.

That's when he rode up a driveway, threw his bike down and ran into the house screaming, "Mom!"

How could I be so stupid?

I never had considered that my riding lesson could look like a two-wheeled kidnapping attempt to my bike guru!

My brain flooded. Fight or flight? Fight or flight? Maybe I could calmly explain to bike guru's mom that I, a fully grown adult, am afraid of riding my bike. No, no, that sounds ridiculous. I should run. But then I'd look guilty. What to do?

I chose flight.

I rode back to my place, quickly chained up the enemy and ran inside my house, locking the doors, afraid to show my face. Mortified.

I think it's time I call Goodwill to schedule a pickup. The bike knows too much.

Safety Patrol

"It was cool. I swear."

Sometimes when my husband laughs, he looks as if he is having a seizure. This would be endearing, if his full-bodied laugh didn't so often occur when he is laughing at me.

"You were such a dweeb," my husband said, clutching his stomach.

"I was not! You had to be popular and authoritative to be given such an honor. It was cool. It was the thing to be in sixth grade."

I was talking, of course, about being a school safety patrol.

Not everyone was made to don the safety patrol uniform, consisting of an orange plastic sash and a metal badge. It was a symbol of sixth-grade status. Of coolness. Of achievement. When I was a kindergartener, I looked up at those orange-clad elementary-school seniors. Their spiffy reflective fabrics ranked them in my upper echelon of awesomeness.

Clearly, my husband didn't understand the prestige that came with reciting the safety patrol oath, because he kept on chuckling. "Did you send kids to detention if they didn't have their hall pass? Narc!"

How dare you?" I asked. "That's a hall monitor. They were the dweebs. A hall monitor and a safety patrol are totally different!"

And my husband convulsed into hysterics.

I began speaking at a Micro Machines man pace, attempting to defend my 12-year-old title, clinging to the social status of my primary years. But as I rambled on, my argument unraveled.

"We'd get out of class early," I said. "Even you have to admit that leaving class is cool." And it was. An early bell rang just for those of us who had taken the pledge to seat and protect. Every day, the other kids in class groaned and moaned that we got to bounce while they had to sit for another 10 full minutes of learning. That's, like, 18 months in kid years.

"Yeah, but does that mean you had to get up early in the mornings, too?"

Drat!

For all the street cred you get for skipping out of class, it is all lost once folks realize you're the loser who has to get out of bed early to hang out at the bus stop before sunrise.

OK, that example didn't exactly work to establish my coolness, but there were other examples, such as the respect. Yeah, the respect! I had authority. I had swagger. I had all those little kids on my bus wrapped around my finger. They would walk in a single line for me. They would stay on the sidewalk. They would keep their voices down. When I told kids to sit down, they'd sit down. When I told them to shut up, they'd shut up.

Well, that is, of course, if you ignore that one infamous time when I asked a third-grader causing trouble to take a seat. To which he politely responded with a right hook. Sure, I had a black eye and a scratched retina, but my heroism earned me a free pass out of school that day -- because my mommy had to take me to the eye doctor.

Oh, how my husband laughed when I told him this. I was beginning to hate his smile.

OK, maybe the authority angle wasn't my best argument. But that's fine. I mean, it's not as if I was a power-hungry kid. I became a safety patrol for the perks. Yeah, you heard right. The perks. At the end of every school year, the county put on a special carnival just for us safety patrols. It was a way of saying "thank you" for all our hard work (and black eyes).

When I mentioned this to my husband, his epileptic giggle attack subsided. Even he could admit that a personalized carnival sounded pretty cool.

"So what kind of rides did they have for you?" he asked.

Well -- drat! I mean, there were rides. Sorta. They had a slide and a carousel, both of which we all felt too old for.

"Did you at least get funnel cake?"

"Um, yes. Of course I did. Yum."

I didn't want to tell him that we had to bring our own lunches.

The years have rusted the prestige of my orange sash. Maybe being a safety patrol wasn't so cool as I remember. But hey, at least I wasn't a hall monitor. Now that would've been embarrassing.

Doppelganger

It all started when my co-worker Bryan was sent a picture of a Vietnam War photographer. The caption beneath the picture said, "You ever travel back in time to be a war photographer?" Bryan, who was decades away from being conceived when the photo was taken, was the spitting image of the man in the picture.

We're not talking about your run-of-the-mill scenario when a person walks up to you in a grocery and says, "You look just like my cousin Ethel, only she has red hair. And a mole on her chin. And is a few hundred pounds heavier than you. And a few feet shorter. And is a vampire." No, this was not your typical smile-and-nod situation. Trust me; if you're inclined to believe in reincarnation, this picture of Bryan before Bryan was born is all the proof you need.

135

It got the rest of my co-workers wondering whether we, too, have doppelgangers. That's when Lily, another co-worker, semi-jokingly said she found her lookalike in the English comedian Stephen Fry. Stephen Fry, as you might have guessed, is a man.

Within seconds, we abandoned all hope and interest in finding our true doppelgangers, as Bryan had found, and instead set forth on a new exploratory adventure.

Turn off the phones! Lock the doors! We have far more pressing work to attend to. We were in search of our opposite-gender doppelgangers!

Well, at least, my co-workers set forth on their searches. For me, no search was required. I knew who my male twin is. His name has been my nickname since I was just a few months old: Willard Scott.

I'd like to think the bulk of the resemblance is because of the twinkle in his eyes or perhaps because of the goofy, effervescent smile that takes over his entire face or because of how his chubby cheeks lend themselves to a friendly accessibility. Sure, my male doppelganger is not the most desirable comparison, but I can find a handful of complimentary reasons behind one's saying I look like Willard Scott.

Sadly, none of those is the reason behind it. My dad came up with the oh-so-flattering nickname because I, like our favorite weatherman, was bald and fat. The sad part is that I never grew out of looking like the man. I may have a bit more hair now, but you can't ignore that we have the same eyes, nose, chin, cheeks, smile and all-encompassing love for canned fruit preserves.

The first time my boyfriend, now husband, heard my dad call me Willard, he proudly and promptly exclaimed, "I see it!"

Yeah, yeah, so do I.

Not that I'm complaining. There are certainly worse people to have as your male doppelganger. Adolf Hitler, for example, would be way worse. Not only would it be bothersome to look like pure evil in human form but also, as a woman, pulling off that mustache would be tricky. Attila the Hun would be a rough comparison. As would Shrek, Jabba the Hutt or Mickey Rourke.

Honestly, I've come to terms with my inner and outer Willard. I may not have the same love for centenarians that he does, but who doesn't love the idea of letting the world know when sunshine is heading its way?

Oh, yes, Willard and I had become one long ago. That is why while others trepidatiously looked into who their opposite-gender doppelganger is, I felt comfortable and secure with my lifelong brother from another mother.

When my co-workers were done identifying their opposite-gender doppelgangers, they all seemed quite pleased. The boys' doppelgangers were Amy Ryan, Eliza Dushku and Chloe Grace Moretz. The girls' doppelgangers were Peter Gallagher, Martin Freeman and, of course, Stephen Fry in drag, who, by the way, makes a very attractive woman.

I announced my male doppelganger is Willard Scott. My co-workers graciously jumped to inform me that he most certainly is not. I smiled. "Yes, he is," I said, and I pulled out the baby photos with which there is no denying it.

"Oh, my gosh," a co-worker said, holding a picture of me. "I'm sorry."

Hey, I may not make an attractive man, but I bet that if I play my cards right, I may be able to get a free lifetime supply of Smucker's jelly. With a face like Willard's, it has to be good.

Lost Keys

My seventh-grade science teacher used to say I'd lose my head if it weren't attached. I always hated that saying. First of all, if your head fell off, you'd have bigger things to worry about than finding your body or anything else you misplaced -- such as that whole being dead thing. I'm fairly certain the Headless Horseman wasn't terrorizing Sleepy Hollow in search of his lost reading glasses. Secondly, I'd like to think that I'd keep tabs on my detachable head. There are plenty of important things I haven't lost -- for example, my car. I may have misplaced it a few (hundred) times in parking lots, but I never have lost my vehicle completely.

That's not to say I haven't come close.

This past week, I headed over to a cute part of town with Michelle, one of my best friends from high school, who was visiting me. I parked the car on a side street, and for the next few hours, we strolled around, grabbing lunch and shopping in cute boutiques.

Back at the car, I felt in my purse for my keys, but I couldn't find them.

"Aren't those your keys?" Michelle asked, pointing to a massive bushel that would make any hotel owner/Scooby Doo villain jealous. My keys had been left in plain sight on the roof of the car. For hours.

I snatched the keys off the roof.

"I'm so glad you're still here!" I exclaimed, hugging the car. "I could've lost you forever."

"You're so lucky," Michelle said.

Before heading to the next stop in our day o' fun, I decided to feed my baby. I sat in the driver's seat, covered up with a blanket, and I picked up the conversation with Michelle that had been interrupted with the discovery of my roof keys. About 20 minutes and four conversation topics later, we were ready to roll.

Hmm, now where did I put those keys?

"Did you leave them on the roof?" Michelle suggested. I got out of the car and checked. Nope.

"In the trunk?" Nope.

"Then they have to be somewhere in the car," Michelle said.

Yes, they have to be somewhere in the car. But where?

My car is an embarrassment. Practically having morphed into a mobile home, my car not only provides transportation but has become the room in which I pump milk from my breasts. Seeing as I have to take pumping breaks during the workday, I usually am finishing papers and eating lunch while I pump. So my car has taken on the cluttered and trashed, albeit homey, feel often ascribed to scary secret dungeons and studio apartments in Manhattan.

If I had lost a single key somewhere in the jungle that is my car, it would've been a lost cause. But my behemoth set of keys could be used as a weapon. I wasn't worried about finding them.

Ten minutes later, I still was looking.

"Oh, the great irony," Michelle said. "You find your keys left on the roof of your car and then lose them once you get inside."

I went through my diaper bag and shopping bags. I picked up or folded or discarded every random particle in my vehicle. The car never looked better, but the keys were nowhere to be found.

Twenty minutes later, the search still was going. I was starting to crack. I did have keys at some point, right? We did see my keys on the roof. I'm not crazy, right?

That's when I saw a friend of mine walking toward my car, a beautiful set of keys dangling from her hand. My keys! Blood rushed to my face. Oh, the joy! Finally, an end to this absurd search! But then rational thinking returned. Those weren't my keys. How could they be? She was just carrying her own set.

I was losing it. I looked. And relooked. And looked again. After 30 minutes of a maddening search, I found the keys stuck in a nook by the passenger seat.

My friend looked amused. I could tell she wanted to comment on how my scatterbrained ways hadn't changed since high school. But to her credit, she didn't say anything. So I did.

"Nice to know nothing changes, huh?"

Michelle smiled and agreed.

My science teacher should've spent less time worrying about me losing my head and more time worried I'd lose my mind.

A Retainer on Baby Food

"Oh, man, apple plum berry is still my favorite," I said to my friend as I scraped the bottom of my son's glass jar of baby food and gingerly lapped up the last of it off my spoon. "I seriously could eat this all day."

My friend wiped food off my son's face and watched me with piqued interest. Perhaps she had never before seen an adult go to town on a baby's unfinished Gerber goodies.

I offered her a spoonful. She shook her head "no."

"It's cool that your tastes haven't changed in all this time," my friend said.

"Yeah. What was your favorite baby food?"

"Oh, I don't know. I doubt my mom remembers," my friend said.

"Yeah," I said. "I bet my mom doesn't remember, either."

"But..." My friend stared at me. Then she asked, "Are you saying that you remember your favorite baby food?"

"I just told you. Apple plum berry."

My friend stared at me incredulously. I stared back, confused. What was her deal?

For me, the best part of my son's moving on to solid foods has been tasting his many jars of baby food. It's nostalgic -- a trip down memory lane. But now, for some reason, my friend was staring at me as if I were either some total bozo or the world's most ridiculous liar.

"So I guess you remember being breast-fed, too, right?" she asked, with more than a hint of sarcasm.

"What? No. Don't be ridiculous!"

"But..." Once again, my friend just stared at me. And I stared back. Then suddenly, it dawned on me where all this confusion was coming from.

"O-o-o-o-o-o-h," I said. "You think that I was a baby when I ate baby food!"

My bad.

I've been told I ate a wide variety of mashed meals in my first few years of life. I'm sure that's true, but I don't remember any of it. What I do remember is the veritable smorgasbord of baby food I ate for a full year when I was 9. Yes, 9.

When I was in third grade, my orthodontist attempted to correct an overbite by placing a retainer in my mouth. It covered all my top teeth and hung down, acting as a tongue guard. Worst of all, it was permanent. It couldn't come out of my mouth. Not at night. Not for special occasions. Not ever -- no how, no way -- unless the removal was performed by the orthodontist.

This retainer was essentially a prepubescent torture device -- all the humiliation of adolescence without the coping mechanism of the aloof attitude acquired at 13. I was simply glued into a clear plastic devastation device and told to suck it up. Not that I could suck. Sucking with that contraption was nearly impossible. In fact, simply closing my mouth was nearly impossible.

To add insult to injury, the permanent retainer made me lose all my friends to my chronic spitting. It's hard to share secrets with your buds when they wind up showered with an earful of your saliva.

Shockingly, becoming an easy target for kids at school and losing my friends weren't the most heinous parts of having the permanent retainer. It had robbed me of the one thing I loved most in this world: eating.

Chewing was awkward and time-consuming and soon became too much work. My new diet consisted of yogurt, pudding, applesauce, soup and good ol' baby food.

If I'm being honest, the baby food was the best thing to come out of my orthodontic nightmare.

It wasn't always easy being the weird kid who brought baby food to school, but I loved going to the grocery with my mom. I loved walking up and down the baby food aisle and picking out exactly what I wanted to eat for every meal for the next few days. There was a newfound autonomy that few kids had at the young age of 9.

Tasting my son's baby food has been a happy reminder of something good in a time that was not. I just have to remember that most people don't have the same accessible nostalgia for Gerber Good Start that I do. And that's too bad, because I'm tellin' ya, the food has only gotten more delicious! Seriously.

Clink your glass jars, and raise your sippy cups! Cheers to the memories!

Clash of the Tile-tans

My clothes have never matched.

I mean, I always thought they did. But the moment I'd arrive at school, I was promptly told otherwise. Via friends. Via teachers. Via the morning announcements over the PA system.

OK, OK, no one made fun of my clothes over the morning announcements, but the unwelcome commentary was pervasive with, well, my entire life experience. I never cared much for how I looked, so the whispers and blatant mockery weren't so much a concern as they were baffling.

Most of my heroes don't match: Pippi Longstocking, Ramona Quimby, my dad. But all those crazy characters knew they were being outrageous, whereas I was just trying to look like your average cool kid/teenager/adult/professional. Once, at work, when I was dressed in an outfit that I thought looked particularly professional and adorable, my boss came up to me and said, "Have you ever heard the saying that you should dress for the job you want, not the job you have? Perhaps you could try implementing that."

I looked down at my clothes. What was wrong with them? My clothes were not tight or short. They were not loud, outrageous or inappropriate. And seeing as how most days I rolled into work in something that looked shockingly close to pajamas (shh, they were pajamas), I assumed I looked far more respectable than usual. When I got home, I asked my husband what he thought of my outfit. He giggled, "It's fine -- other than the fact that you clash horribly."

There was that word again: clash. My arch-nemesis of words. My husband was laughing so hard that I couldn't help but laugh, too, but as I looked down at my outfit, I didn't see anything that clashed. In fact, I don't think I've experienced what "clashing" looks like.

A few times on days when I've been drenched by a wave of fashion insults, I've found myself looking around for Ashton Kutcher to jump out from some bush, laughing his stupid face off. But that hasn't happened, and even in my most vain and self-absorbed moments, of which there have been plenty, I have never been quite able to convince myself that my life is a "Truman Show" type of conspiracy with my fashion choices at the crux of the show's high ratings. Though, now that I'm thinking about it again...

A number of years ago, I was given a vision quiz and discovered that I actually cannot see the hues. The smaller variations among colors are lost on me. Clashing is an impossibility.

In the wake of whether the dress is blue and black or white and gold, I have never been more aware of my lack of color clarity. And now, this week, I am being met with my biggest color challenge.

Our roof is falling apart, and we are at risk of turning into an aquarium by next rainfall. In the whirlwind that has been our lives lately, my husband and I forgot we needed to pick the new color for our roof. Now he is on a work trip, and I, the colorblind-ish one, am left alone to make a multi-thousand-dollar decision.

(Enter hyperventilation here.) I can't do this alone! Somebody needs to help me! I don't want to spend thousands of dollars on a roof that will clash with my house for the next 30 years! I sent my husband a text message in a panic. He simply wrote back, "I trust you."

"I trust you"? Are you crazy?! I didn't just ask an easy question, such as what flavor ice cream I should bring home from the store, whether I would look good in bangs or whether we should get a divorce -- perhaps not typically an easy question but one that seems exceptionally obvious in this moment.

I called a few good friends and asked them to drive around to look at roofs and pick colors that would match my house -- one that I describe as orange but others claim is a peach color. (As if it's not the same exact thing!) No one was available.

So I guess it's just me. Colorblind-ish me. It's not a big deal if the house clashes with the roof, right? It's just 30 years of my life and resale value on the line. If I survived junior high, I can survive snarky neighbors.

Maybe I'll just paint yellow stripes and purple circles on the house. WWPD? (What would Pippi do?)

The Onion Dare

"Katiedid will drink it."

"Oh, will I?" I asked. My high-school friends meet once a year in a new locale. It gives us an excuse to take a cheap vacation and see one another. This year, we went to Las Vegas. "That's funny, because I don't remember saying I wanted to vomit today."

We had ordered the sampler platter at the Coca-Cola store and had mixed all the disgusting Coke drinks from around the world into one menacing cup.

"The Katiedid I used to know wouldn't even hesitate to take on a dare," my friend taunted.

Game on.

My high-school group of friends was compiled of good girls. We didn't drink. We barely dated. To pass the time, we played truth or dare. Well, really dare or dare. And I was never one to turn down a dare.

The day of my Homecoming dance, my friends dared me to eat a whole onion like an apple. I know what you're thinking: "Please, tell me that you did not take on this most daring-dare-of-dares."

The stinging tears streaming down my face were completely worth the $5 I earned by conquering such a fantastical feat. The only thing left to prove such an onion ever existed was my gnarly, fabulous breath. That's the smell of pride, ladies and gentlemen. Pure pride.

Before the dance, I brushed my teeth six times. I drank so much Listerine that I was a little loaded. Move over, spiked punch bowl; I had tartar control getting me high.

At dances, I usually wall-flowered it, standing off to the side with my friends, gossiping about the kids in my class. But this Homecoming, my crush, Jackson, asked me to dance.

So dance I did.

I danced with reckless abandon. My sweaty hair was plastered across my face.

Jackson and I only slowed down our dancing nuptials when we ... sorta ... got an odd ... whiff ... of something coming from the gym's dance floor. *What is that?!*

Strangely enough, the more I danced the stronger that smell became. Until (SNIFF) until (SNIFF) oh, man, that smell is coming from me!

I looked at the "father of my future children" and gave him a weak smile, trying to mask my horror.

I stood there, looking for a way out as the raw onion seeped out of my skin, through my pores, across my forehead, down my chest and under my armpits. Lines of pungent onion sweat were everywhere.

I tried to blame the smell on something else. Anything else. But the look on Jackson's face said everything. He knew the funk came from yours truly.

My onion challenge had ruined any chance I ever had with Jackson, but it also gave my friends years of laughter recounting that night. And here they were again, 10 years later, with a disgusting dare sitting in front of me.

They offered me $5. I wavered. They raised it to $10.

I could guess what would follow if I took the dare: a rank taste in my mouth, possibly vomiting or a stomachache that'd cramp up when we were out dancing.

Strangers at the table next to ours caught on to the drink dare. Impressed anyone would consider drinking something so foul, they added another $10 into the pot. So $20 to drink something that smelled like rotten carcasses.

"I just don't want to be sick for our rare weekend together" I said.

"We understand. Everyone changes," said my friend Emily. Ouch. That hurt.

I looked down at that brown drink. Then I looked at my smiling friends. I couldn't be positive this drink would give me a stomachache or make me vomit. After all, people around the world paid money to drink Coke products. I couldn't be sure my breath would stink or that my head would ache or that I would get the sweats. But what I could be sure of was years' worth of stories and laughter that would come from this final dare. That was a definite.

I pocketed the $20.

I chugged the rancid beverage as my friends and a table of strangers cheered.

I used the $20 to buy Tums.

Totally worth it.

~ ~ ~

Chapter 10

There Is a Season, Turn, Burn, Yearn: Changes

Gold Nuggets of Wisdom

I never would have guessed that one of the most defining moments of my life would be a moonlit midnight stroll on the beach with a homeless man. Funny how life works out.

In the months that followed college graduation, I bought a one-way plane ticket, leaving behind a boyfriend and the looming question of whether it was time to move in together or move on from each other. Hoofing around Europe was the perfect distraction from all the things I was too afraid to face. My future, my relationship, my career. Myself. Monoliths at home, these fears were easily ignored standing in the shadow of the Eiffel Tower. The months gave way to the illusion that I could escape them forever; that's when I met Giovanni.

Sicily is home to active volcanoes. Hardened black magma coats the coastline, acting as a constant reminder that we are never safe from what is boiling under the surface.

I first saw Giovanni when I stepped off the ferry into a rainy night on the Italian island. He was cheerfully busking, playing his violin. I averted eye contact and began my 2-mile trek through a torrential downpour toward my hostel. When I arrived in my room, there he was again -- my new bunkmate.

Cold, tired, dripping wet and irritated to be sharing my room with a homeless man, I behaved decidedly aloof. But Giovanni was impossible to ignore.

A Persian Parisian, Giovanni moved from Iran to Paris when he was 10. A dozen years later, he moved to Texas to make his fortune and fell head over stirrups for a cowgirl. He loved her, married her, worshipped her, was cuckolded by her and divorced her. It was then, Giovanni admitted, that he went a little crazy.

"Now I'm a troubadour," he said, showing me pages of stamps in his passport. "I go where the music takes me. I play my violin, and I make people smile."

"But you're homeless."

"Earth is my home. When it's warm, I listen to her crashing waves and fall asleep on her sands."

"And when it's cold?"

"I come inside and meet pleasant folks like you." And he winked.

In no time, I was living in Giovanni-land. We danced in the salted sea mist. Forged through fog toward mountaintops. Broke in to a five-star hotel at midnight and played music in the courtyard as guards chased us around, eventually succeeding in physically removing us from the premises.

Days of laughter spilled into weeks. "You know what your problem is?" Giovanni asked one night while we were taking a moonlit walk, inspecting the burnt sands of the island. "You're so focused on this," he said as he picked up a volcanic rock and handed it to me, "you're forgetting to show the world this." Giovanni turned my hand over, exposing the bright red underbelly of the rock. "Don't hide your colors, princess."

I looked at him, awestruck. Speechless.

"Come. Let's make some people smile." And he winked.

It was the night before St. Nicholas Day. Giovanni and I spent the early hours before dawn spraying rocks with gold paint and leaving them on doorsteps for children to find in the morning. Sun was breaking as we completed our deliveries.

When I woke, Giovanni wasn't in the bunk below mine. I went to our meeting spot and watched little children dancing with delight upon discovering their golden gifts.

Giovanni never showed up, and I kinda knew he wouldn't. He was like the gold nuggets we had delivered. Everything that shone and glistened was just a thin coat hiding a black, hardened core. Giovanni was spontaneous and fun, but his every action was simply a reaction to a heart broken, to a soul lost. He, too, did not know what was coming next in his life. The only real difference between Giovanni and me was that I had a home waiting for me.

It was time to book my return flight.

Walking toward the Internet cafe, I flipped the rock Giovanni had given me in my hand as one would a two-sided coin, looking to it for guidance on whether I should risk my heart, take a chance and move in with my boyfriend (the man who has since become my husband and the father of my child). The rock flipped from red to black. From black to red. To red. Red. Red. Red. Red. Red.

146

A Hostel Situation

As we age, there is an inevitable loss and longing for the person we once were. It's why 6-year-olds suddenly put pacifiers back in their mouths. Why 60-year-olds buy back the sports car of their youth. It's why I went to San Francisco.

When I was 19, I spent a year backpacking Oceania. Hostels were home. I was immersed in cultures from around the world, sang songs in different languages, lived on $12 a day for food and accommodations. It became a lifestyle. I identified as a backpacker.

Since then, I've had stints in being a backpacker again, but the duration has never been so long. Recently, my travel itch was becoming insatiable. I wanted to recapture the poor, carefree, haven't-showered-in-a-week, ramen-loving backpacker that I knew was still buried in there somewhere.

I didn't have the money or the time off to go on vacation, but a three-day weekend was coming up. Having never before stayed in an American hostel, I decided now was the time.

This hostel was like none I ever had stayed at. Rather than have up to 20 bunk beds in a single room, this hostel had two queens -- for four people. It was, essentially, just an overbooked hotel. Not only were you required to share a bed with a stranger but also the bed sagged so severely that even in full wakefulness, it was nearly impossible for me not to roll on top of my new bedmate. Call me old-fashioned, but I prefer to know your name before you're snoring on top of me.

It was midnight, and I was unintentionally spooning my bedmate, when two girls from the U.K., meant to sleep in the queen next to my co-occupied one, came in, dragging their monster-sized suitcases. They flipped on the light and spoke at full volume. I was going to tell them to be quiet, but I reconsidered. Hostels were always like this, and I loved hostels, right? I'm still a backpacker, aren't I? I put in earplugs and fell asleep, presumably on top of my bedmate.

The next morning, I got an early start to the day. My British roommates were still fast asleep as I tiptoed around the room and left for a day of hiking through Muir Woods.

When I got back, the British girls had completely taken over the room. They ran around, curling their hair, trying on different clubbing outfits.

147

"Aren't you going out?" one asked me.

"No, I'm really tired."

They looked at me with a mix of pity and horror.

As they walked out, I noticed they were leaving their passports and phones on the bed.

"You may want to take those with you."

"Our outfits don't have pockets."

"But it's your first night in a foreign country. You'll need identification. What if you get lost? You'll want your phone."

The girls laughed at me and walked out.

Oh, to be young and stupid again.

At 4 a.m., the British girls came stumbling back into the room.

They flipped on the lights and their volume.

"Did you like Michael?"

"He was so-o-o-o- cute."

"And good in bed. Was your guy good in bed?"

"Yeah. I wish I got his name."

Good grief.

I threw the pillow over my head and sank into the center of my bed.

When I got back from breakfast the next morning, the British girls were gone, but their phones and passports were still on the bed.

I thought of me at 19. I'm positive there were times when I was that jerk in the hostel, turning on lights and stomping around. But these girls felt so far away from me. So unrelatable. I needed to know their ages.

I picked up the passports. One girl was six months younger than I am. The other girl was three days older.

And that's when it hit. It's not my age that makes me too old to party and pack and behave as they did. I just personally have grown past that point. Way, way past that point. And knowing this was both incredibly depressing and fantastically freeing.

I spent my last night in San Francisco on a hard, flat mattress in a bed all to myself -- at the Holiday Inn.

Wanderlust

I've been mainlining "House Hunters International."

A steady shot straight to the gut of what my life could be. Sandy beaches. Outdoor cafes. Wine at twilight. Monkeys ravaging my luggage, wearing my underwear. Pet dolphins eating Cap'n Crunch out of the palm of my hand. Me eating Cap'n Crunch out of the palm of my hand.

There is danger in watching a Sunday marathon of "House Hunters International." You start to lose your sense of reality. A new country every 30 minutes. A new lifestyle different from your own. The pulsating energy of city lights. The breathless silence of isolated desert. Before you know it, the sun is down, and you're not sure whether you're ordering a new passport to become a cheese-maker in Chile, a kite surfer in South Africa or a nudist sculptor in Florence. The only thing you are certain of is that you are moving. It's only a matter of time before you naturally develop an exotic accent and a classy birthmark on your left cheek and adopt a miniature poodle with a lion cut whose coat naturally changes color to match whichever wine you're drinking.

I'm suffering from wanderlust.

Perhaps it's because I stay home more often since having my son. Nowadays, the most exotic place I go is the Panda Express at the mall food court. Chopsticks in hand, I try my best to imagine I'm staring at the Forbidden City, but when I open my eyes, it's just a Frederick's of Hollywood. Instead of flying around the world in 80 days, I push a stroller around the 80 carts selling hair bands and cellphone cases. Sure, my toddler loves jumping on the octopus-shaped slide and driving the foam boat in the mall's kiddie section, but one aquarium does not a scuba trip in the Caymans make.

I used to be interesting. I find myself saying that a lot lately. With two years of backpacking under my belt and work as an adventure tour guide in the Outback on my resume, I used to be interesting. On second thought, perhaps the better word is reckless.

For as much time as I have spent living abroad, it was never lived in the formal fashion of "House Hunters International." I spent months eating only a single baguette a day, hitchhiking, rock climbing without ropes, sleeping in tents, sleeping on park benches, sleeping in strangers' homes and doing just about everything that I, now as a mom, will use my every last breath to try to deter my child from doing.

It's a weird feeling becoming a parent. On one hand, I've never felt more connected. Here is this person whom I created, who owns my heart, whom I breathe for. But on the other hand, I've never felt less connected to the person I identify as being, and I haven't yet figured out how to be both. Folks didn't like it when Steve Irwin wrangled a crocodile while holding his baby. Back then, I thought that as long as the Crocodile Hunter hadn't lathered up his baby in goose fat before entering the crocodile den, he was fine. My perspective has changed.

Previously, I spent nights out of my tent, sleeping under the stars, as a pack of dingoes attacked a baby calf less than 100 feet away. Now I'll ask a dog walker how friendly her 12-week-old puppy is before I let my son pet him. Previously, I would have seen white windowless vans as little more than a nice place to sleep on rainy nights. These days, my son's obsession with windowless vans, including a knack for running to their back doors, has me a tad bit nervous. Everything I do now errs on the side of safety. Everything I do now errs on the side of boring.

Even my fantasies have become dull. When I watch "House Hunters International," I find myself ticking off certain locations because of their risk ratios. Australia has too many snakes. Brazil has too many waves. Samoa has a ridiculously delicious Girl Scout cookie named after it, sure to cause diabetes and end in the amputation of limbs.

I thought I'd be crunchier than this. More granola. Not that I'd ever actually eat granola; I'm not that crazy.

Perhaps it is time to turn off the TV and dust off the ol' tent. There may be too many waves in Brazil, but there aren't any in my backyard.

Adventuring Onto a New Career Path

There comes a time in every woman's life when she must look at the choices she has made and ask herself whether she is living her best life. After careful consideration and a lot of soul-searching, I've decided that I am ready to pursue a different career path. This decision didn't come easily, and I hope I can rely on all of your support as I venture into my new occupation as ... a filthy-rich aristocrat.

Enough of this dillydallying with money and bills. In my new career as the executor to my own immense wealth, I will "work" at trying to find new and creative ways to spend my boatloads of cash.

To start, I must buy boats and physically load them with cash. I'm confident it will be smooth sailing from there.

Always an advocate of education, I will focus my new career on putting money toward logical and attainable scientific undertakings, such as mating the Tasmanian devil and a tiger to genetically re-engineer the extinct Tasmanian tiger. I will become the founder and CEO of new charities, such as the Make Purple Finches Purple Foundation. We've been mocked long enough by that red bird, and once I get promoted to aristocrat, I'm not going to take it anymore! And is it just me, or does a closetful of sweaters made from dandelion fluff seem like a must-have in every classroom?

In my new occupation, I will remain blissfully unaware of small matters such as rent, the mortgage and the cost of my custom-ordered Aston Martin, made entirely of bamboo and fueled by gluten-free spaghetti. I will wade in my swimming pool vault of gold coins, but unlike Scrooge McDuck, I will be a benevolent aristocrat -- better than the Crawley family of "Downton Abbey." I'll hire a maid for my maid's maid and a cook to make dinner for my chef's family. I'll write enormously oversize checks to important political campaigns, such as Bring Back the Telegram.

Don't let my excitement over my new career give you the wrong idea. Deciding whether to become an aristocrat was a heart-rending experience. I love my job. But I knew it was time to begin combing Craigslist for positions of ridiculous wealth when something devastating pushed me over the edge. Last Friday, I was sitting at my desk, typing away, when I realized it wasn't Friday. It was Monday. A devastating blow so early in the workweek. It felt like Friday because I had worked all weekend, catching up on side projects and cleaning my house.

That night, while rocking my baby to sleep, I found myself apologizing to him for being absent. I had barely seen him the week before because of long work hours, and the weekend had been spent on chores rather than on peekaboo.

It was time for an Oprah moment. Time to re-evaluate my life's decisions. Whoever says money doesn't buy happiness doesn't understand simple mathematics. Happiness may not be for sale, but time is. Money buys time. Free time creates happiness. Therefore, money buys happiness. This is simple if-A-equals-B-and-B-equals-C-then-A-equals-C stuff. I may have almost failed sixth-grade math, but I understand this equation.

The problem is that I have searched job websites for nearly a week now but haven't seen any openings to become a person of immense wealth. I tried reaching out to my alma mater's career center to see whether anyone there knew of any internships that would help me get my foot in the door of the aristocracy, but no one has responded to my email. I'm sure everyone is just busy.

Last night, I Googled Kim Kardashian's contact information so I could ask her how she got her first aristocrat gig. Surprisingly, her number is unlisted. Maybe I should try G-chatting Paris Hilton.

Truth be told, I feel as if I'm in a race against the clock. It will only be so long until other people have the same epiphany I did and decide to pursue their own careers in simply being wealthy. I will have competition! If I'm being serious about my future career, I have to be proactive about making it happen. Next month, I'm going to Las Vegas and putting it all down on red. Guaranteed immense wealth. I can't believe no one's thought of this! New career, here I come!

A Penny Stolen Is a Penny Earned

Last week, I wrote about my new desired vocation as an aristocrat. Sadly, since my column went out, not one of you lovely readers has contacted me with a job offer. I can't say I'm not a little disappointed in all of you. I'm not angry; I'm just hurt.

Maybe my dream of becoming rich Uncle Pennybags overnight was slightly overambitious (especially considering the surgery involved). Two whole weeks have gone by, and I still haven't seen any job openings on Craigslist for a wannabe aristocrat. Also, my attempts at trying to fake it till I make it have fallen short. Perhaps I need to expand my research on how to behave like the top 1 percent past binging on marathons of Paris Hilton's "The Simple Life" and Disney's "The Aristocats."

In the interim, while I wait for my Las Vegas trip to pay off and the winning lottery ticket to come in, I've decided to proactively work toward creating my own desired future with an entrepreneurial endeavor. And I'm going to do it the right way, too. The fair way. With honesty. Integrity. And maybe just a pinch of thievery.

My soon-to-be-Fortune 500 idea came to me when I was out to lunch with a mommy friend of mine. She had just put her newly walking 1-year-old on the restaurant floor. In no time, the little man was toddling from chair to chair. Most patrons looked over at him for a split second, smiled and went back to their personal conversations, ignoring the baby pulling on the back of their seats. The restaurant-goers who did pay attention to the adorable toddling baby said things such as, "Aren't you precious." And they didn't change their verbiage one iota when this little boy began digging through the purses hanging from their chairs! He took out wallets. Dangled keys. And if the patron noticed, if she said anything at all, it was simply: "Remember them like this. Time flies."

Voila! A new business was born! Babies sveltely stealing from eye-level personables!

I call my new business Baby Bandits. It won out by a slight margin over Toddler Thievery, Kiddie Crooks and Pint-size Pickpockets. Though, if you come up with something better, I am open to suggestions.

The business will start small. I'm enlisting my friend's child into the rigorous Baby Bandits training process. Sadly, my own son is proving to be quite a disappointing delinquent; he can't even walk yet. I still am holding out hope for his future.

Once my son and his friend rake in enough cash, I will open Baby Bandits School. There I will charge for classes and demand commission on every job. We'll take it slowly, careful not to over-expand the business. But don't worry; I'm sure franchise opportunities will be coming soon for all of you.

Baby Bandits School will focus on teaching all the important steps: purse profiling, brand names versus knockoffs (these babies may not know the alphabet, but they will recognize the double C for Chanel!), and identifying the adults who are the most involved in conversations and the least likely to pay attention to a wallet-stealing whippersnapper. Acting lessons also will be part of the formal training. Smiling innocently and dramatizing a wet, drooling giggle will be on the final exam.

Parents also are encouraged to enroll in Baby Bandits School. It was very clear to me that the reason no one was upset when my friend's baby rummaged through purses was my friend looked mortified when she apologized. At Baby Bandits School, I will bottle that reaction and teach it to all of the parents in a method acting intensive.

The best part of Baby Bandits is that it is a mere dip into the crime pool. The window of time when your baby needs support walking and can get away with pulling on the back of chairs is so short that it is nearly impossible to get stuck in this lifestyle. Another benefit of Baby Bandits is that it is open to everyone. If your kid is too funny-looking to be a baby model, save for her college education by putting her to work as a swindling 7-month-old. She will earn all the same money without acquiring a bad body image.

Clearly, this is a multimillion-dollar idea just waiting to happen. Time to patent my pint-size pickpocketing project.

Aristocracy, here I come!

Trivia Night

I hate trivia. I would rather carry on a conversation with some bro about perfecting the application of Axe body spray than publicly expose my idiocy all in the name of competitive camaraderie. But this time, trivia night was my idea.

Recently, my high-school foursome of friends connected over Facebook. It had been years since we all had seen one another -- or even spoken, really -- and we were looking to rectify that. A few months and airplane trips later, two of my girls were within an hour's drive of my house, wondering where we could go for a mini reunion on a Tuesday night.

I texted them the address of a tiny South African dive bar that serves savory samosas and has Shock Top on tap. I blamed my postpartum post-partying lifestyle for being unable to direct this reunion to a more hoppin' locale. But in truth, trivia night sounded like a fun way to keep conversation going if our group banter lulled from lack of practice over the years.

The trivia announcer asked the first question.
Name the nightclub Zack Morris got a fake ID to sneak into.

My friends and I looked at one another, stumped. If there is one thing we should know everything about, it's "Saved by the Bell." The night was off to a bad start.
Before we knew it, we were negative points.

`"Zoe should be here," my friend said as we clinked glasses. "She'd have known the answer."

The final member of our foursome was missing. Zoe was across the country, getting acquainted with her newborn baby. When talk of a reunion began, Zoe had been oddly noncommittal. It was after

154

another couple of months, when she announced that she was in her second trimester, that we understood why.

Who was Peter Gabriel's song "In Your Eyes" written about?

Negative 10 points.

I looked around the table at the matured faces of my old friends. We were at such different places in our lives, our relationships, our education, our careers, our child rearing. In a way, it felt almost fitting Zoe was missing the reunion. Even back in high school, the four of us had seemed to exist on vastly different planes, somehow colliding in Zoe's basement.

What is Clippers coach Doc Rivers' first name?

Negative 40 points.

"Do you remember the list we made at senior beach week of where we thought each of us would be in 10 years?" my friend asked, toasting us for the fourth time.

"Oh, yeah," responded my other friend. "Wasn't one of us supposed to be dead in a ditch somewhere by now?"

"That was me, you jerks," I reminded them. And they laughed.

"I'm sure we had a good reason. Starving artist or something. Who kept the list?"

It was Zoe, of course.

What is the name of a baby turkey?

We were down 60 points when we decided to text Zoe.

It was past 2 a.m. on the East Coast, but we told ourselves that she would be awake with her newborn, that she would be happy to hear from us. But when we looked her up in our contact lists, among the three of us, we had four different phone numbers for Zoe.

"Text 'em all!" my friend said as we clinked our glasses for the seventh time.

So we did. We texted her messages I imagine we would have sent one another at 16 if there were such a thing back then. We sent guilt texts. Profane texts. Silly texts. Perverted texts. We texted the four different numbers, knowing full well that we had lost sight of one another so drastically that we did not know which number was hers. We texted, knowing that perhaps none was still hers.

It was midnight. I had work the next day and a sleeping baby to get home to. And two hours into the game, we hadn't gotten a single trivia question right. I considered calling it a night.

But then...

In which month do Canadians celebrate Thanksgiving?

155

"October!" we all yelled out. Zoe was from Canada, and we had spent Canadian Thanksgivings at her house. For a moment, it felt as if Zoe were there with us.

We were still down 50 points and one friend, but our trivia night reunion felt good -- better than those on the receiving end of our mis-sent texts, I'm sure.

Vegas Baby

We stepped into the elevator on the 17th floor and pushed the button to head down to the casino. Stuffed in the elevator car with us were an affluent couple heading to the pool, two wannabe cougars -- their caked-on makeup and skimpy dresses unable to hide the decades of hard living -- and a California "bro" in his early 20s, wasted out of his mind.

It was 10 a.m.

"Who brings a baby to Vegas?" slurred the bro, his animated gesticulations almost hitting me as he questioned my parenting skills. "It's, like, supposed to be 'Vegas, baby.' Ya know? Not 'Vegas *baby*.' Vegas, baby!"

"Yeah," I said, "but he's awesome at blackjack."

The wannabe cougars cackled, unleashing the stench of alcohol on their breath. "Man, I need a drink," said the bro.

"You mean another drink?" asked the affluent pool-bound man.

"Ha-ha, yeah, man. Another. My coke bender is wearing off."

The elevator doors opened, much to my relief. Freedom!

When my husband and I decided to start trying to have a baby, my husband surprised me by having my college group of friends fly into Las Vegas for a long weekend. It was the perfect place to go crazy before a new category of crazy set in. We were loud, drunk, obnoxious. We laughed; we cried; we fought; we hugged. It was the perfect friends weekend.

Now that I was back, baby in tow, I experienced Sin City differently.

Unwilling to walk around in the intense desert heat outside and unable to walk around inside the hotel (babies are not allowed near gambling), we did what I assume most families in Vegas do. We headed to the pool.

En route, we passed the bro from the elevator, who was asking four backpackers from the U.K. whether he could buy hallucinogenic mushrooms from them. Though I ridiculed the bro's idiocy, I couldn't help but wonder whether I ever was this guy.

In Vegas, more than any other place, I find myself doing a personal check. Who am I? Which group of people do I currently fit into? Nearly every time I've gone, my Vegas archetype has changed.

Sin City takes all types. It attracts the rich. The poor. The hard-core partyers. The has-been hard-core partyers. The cultured. The bumpkins. The conservative. The flamboyant. Brides-to-be intermix with women celebrating independence after signing their divorce papers. And unlike the case with any other city I've been to, in Las Vegas, the groups rub shoulders with one another.

My son and I got a front-row seat to view the culture collage as we splashed around in the hotel pool next to patrons holding beer bottles just above the chlorinated water. When they remembered.

Elevator bro had now found his way into the water, approached a group of businessmen and splashed them. A screaming match ensued, with each side threatening to beat up the other. The partying patrons scattered to the edges of the pool. They began yelling at the fighters to stop. Pleading with them. Someone near us screamed, "Stop! There are babies in the pool!"

It was about as tense as a fight can get in the middle of a brightly colored swimming pool in the midday sun. When the fight broke up, the pool patrons applauded. My baby applauded, too. And then people applauded my baby.

Another young family swam over to us, and we began chatting. Their baby was just a day younger than mine. That's when I found a new group of Vegas-goers I never had noticed before: the middle group.

The middlers are the group of people you belong to while transitioning from the Vegas extremes. The folks who are no longer hard-core partyers but are too young to be has-beens. The folks transitioning from poor to rich, from paying college loans to creating college funds. The folks between celebrating their pending marriage and celebrating their final divorce. And for the foreseeable future, they are my Vegas archetype.

After dinner, instead of hitting the clubs, the streets, the bars or anything else delightfully sinful, we headed back up to the 17th floor to watch a Seth Rogen movie on TV and go to bed. On our way up, we passed by the elevator bro, who was wearing a sports jacket and sporting a girl on each arm.

157

Vegas takes all kinds -- even a lame-o like me. It's Vegas, baby.

All Aboard the Doughnut Train

O cursed coveted confectionary, why do you taunt me so?

While traipsing around the East Coast last week, I was reunited with all the sweet treats of my childhood -- candy bars, cakes, chips and drinks that exist solely along the regional line from New York City to Washington, D.C. Tastykakes and Old Bay potato chips called my name, but none yelled more loudly than the local doughnut shops.

Perhaps it was the season -- with Labor Day weekend bringing summer to a close, anointing the era of autumn with apple fritters, apple cider doughnuts ánd maple glaze, sending those sweet, sugary smells into the atmosphere and challenging me to taste the difference between the pumpkin-flavored doughnuts and the pumpkin pie-flavored doughnuts. Naturally, my instinct was to buy all fall flavors. How else would we know which cake reigns supreme? This is important information that must be documented. *Somebody* has to do it.

Or perhaps it was the reason for my trip, the wedding of my beloved cousin, that made me so nostalgic for childhood snacks. Giving hugs to long-lost relatives whom I had most recently seen riding on the handlebars of my bike. Clinking glasses with cousins and dancing with their children whom I had just met. It was fun and beautiful and sad and complicated. And let's be honest; nothing satiates a weekend of family quite like stuffing your face with a fistful of doughnut holes.

My visit back east was a whirlwind, three cities in one week, a local doughnut shack greeting me at every train stop along the way. Never having the time to stop what I was doing and purchase one, I obsessed over the options, circling the circular snacks in my mind. As each day passed, the longing grew stronger. What to choose? What to choose?

This obsession had a familiar taste.

In elementary school, we briefly studied Colonial times and were treated at the end of the study cycle with doughnuts that we made in the classroom. I rolled dough and mixed different sugar, salt and cinnamon combinations in brown paper bags. Delicious aromas filled the air. My stomach gnawed, and it took all my young willpower to stop from reaching into the pots of bubbling oil and pulling out a hot, floating ball of deliciousness all for myself. But I was victorious over the gut growling. I fought the urge and waited patiently as the names of my classmates were called to pick up their delicious homemade delectable doughnuts. I waited. And waited. And waited. As the names of all my classmates were called. Every name. Except mine.

My teacher didn't like me very much.

Now, 20 years later, being banned from binging at bakeries fed off the pain of the past and made my doughnutless existence nearly unbearable. I was screaming on the inside. *You cannot keep me away! I can have strawberry icing and rainbow sprinkles anytime I want! I am an adult!*

Heading toward the last leg of my trip, I finally had the chance to indulge. I walked into the doughnut shop, sized up my options. The classics. The seasonal. The specialties. Weighing which was worth the weight gain. Ultimately, I landed on my old childhood staple: blueberry. It was the favorite from my preteen days, when I had grown past the sprinkles but had not yet morphed into the minimalist glazed doughnut of my teen years. It was a nostalgic choice, from back when I got a doughnut after soccer practice, not before an exam with a cup of coffee. Back when life was simple.

No bag necessary, I insisted, nearly manhandling the treat out of the cashier's hands. Stepping outside, I took a moment to breathe deeply and appreciate this sacred moment I'd waited so long for. Then ... the bite.

Gross!

When do we get too old for the things we love?

For years, I blamed new recipes or ingredients, but the truth is that my taste buds have changed. I simply cannot handle the sweets of my youth anymore. The blueberry doughnut had gone the direction of Cadbury eggs, Fun Dip and Double Bubble.

Is growing up past the taste for Pixy Stix a metaphor for life? Nothing gold can stay?

I walked back into the shop, threw my doughnut into the garbage bin and ordered a coffee.

Medium Pulp

It was one of those rare special evenings. The kind you wish you could plan for, but just as with a star shooting across the night sky, you never can predict the moment your night will light up with wonder and possibility. My 19-month-old had given us the gift of falling asleep early and was tucked soundly in his crib. This was our moment.

The mood was set. The timing was right. Waiting for me in the bedroom, my husband had turned down the covers.

I slid into bed. He put his arms around me and said, "The store had orange juice with medium pulp."

An uncontrollable gasp escaped as I squealed, "They never have orange juice with medium pulp anymore!"

"I know," my husband said, just as enthused. "It's always heavy pulp or pulp-free. I bought two, babe."

I was excited. My husband was excited. And as he kissed my forehead, I hoped aloud that I would have exotic dreams of orange groves and freshly squeezed juice. I looked to my husband; he was already asleep. The excitement for my night of fantasy slumber among the citrus fruit trees waned. Good grief, I thought.

It's official; we're an old married couple.

I was crestfallen. Finding out the tooth fairy isn't real didn't even come close to the full-bodied devastation I felt about the status of my marriage at that moment. Honestly, nothing has come close! Not the pubescent discovery of stray hairs growing on my toes. (I mean, ew!) Not learning that delicious blue cheese is just mold. (We've been eating mold, people! Double ew!) Not even that unspeakable time in my teenage years when an unlocked door led to the ultra-disturbing realization that my parents have sex. (Like, more than just the two times when they conceived children. Ew times infinity!) Even that horrific mental image paled in comparison with the distress of my current situation.

I wanted to shake my husband back into wakefulness and yell, "No, no, we're too young to be this old!" But I knew that he gets cranky if he gets woken up and is likelier to snore if he is disturbed from slumber. Man, we're so old!

Watching my husband sleeping, I looked to the universe for a sign that our pillow talk had not forever turned into a grocery list. That my version of sexting wouldn't be reduced to a text stating that I need a plumber to unclog the drain and meaning it literally. That my idea of a dirty message on Snapchat would include my holding

160

up two diapers in different sizes and asking, "Which one?" The universe didn't respond.

How did we let this happen? Was it because our bathroom door broke?

I began thinking about all the things that get me excited these days. Edible bubbles, attachable drink holders on strollers. Learning that a baby in his car seat qualifies me for the car pool lane brought more uninhibited joy than all my travels, my wedding day and the birth of my child combined. If I had known about the car pool lane thing earlier, I would've gotten pregnant years ago!

And let's not forget, medium-pulp orange juice. Can we all just take a moment and hail all that is wondrous about this juice. Pulp-free is about as natural as boneless chicken wings. Heavy pulp feels like a meal and gets stuck in the spout of my toddler's sippy cup. But medium pulp gives you the crisp and satisfying feeling that you are eating fruit without all the work. Everything in life should be as easy and as delicious as medium-pulp orange juice.

I looked over at the bedside table, where my husband had left me a glass of juice to have before bed. Maybe this wasn't the end of the world.

I met the man whom I now most often refer to as "Daddy" when I was 19 years old. I thought he looked dangerous. (He's not.) Like a bad boy. (Nope.) And I thought he could teach me a thing or two. And he has. He has taught me patience, as he gets up every night to pace our sleep-resistant child back to bed. And support, as he nurtures my ambitions and our child's. And that when a man sees the elusive medium-pulp orange juice at the grocery, if he really loves you, he buys two.

Overachieving

When the paramedics were called, I realized that my efforts to relive my college years perhaps had gone too far.

I've always been an overachiever in the most ridiculous ways. I'm not referring to obsessively removing milkweed from the garden for lactose-intolerant butterflies. That would require using my superpowered hyper-focusing ability for good. I only switch gears into overachiever drive in efforts to be contrary.

When my professors would ask for a 10-page paper proving their set point of view, I would hand in a 20-page paper disproving it.

161

Double the work, double the grade deduction. I may be history's only overachiever who does extra work to fail.

Last week, I returned to the classroom, attending the Erma Bombeck Writers' Workshop at the University of Dayton. This time at college, I came ready to listen, to learn, to write my assigned papers for the assigned number of pages and to go into overachiever overdrive by partying like the Mad Hatter on steroids.

Only an hour's drive from where I attended Miami University, I went against the consensus to rest during my free time from the conference and instead used this first trip away from my baby to do double duty: enhance my adult vocation by day, enhance my alcohol tolerance with old college friends by night.

After a full day of seminars and workshops, I'd return to my college pal's apartment by 10 p.m., hit the bars until 4 a.m. and wake up at 6 a.m. to do it again. Folks said it was impossible. That I would burn out. Pass out. "Leave the partying for the undergrads. You're a mom now."

I've always been an overachiever in the most ridiculous ways.

I needed to show the world I could be it all. To justify still owning a pair of hooker boots. To see 4 a.m. because I wanted to watch the sunrise, not because I was woken by a gassy baby. To prove to myself, even if it was just for a few days, that I could still walk that line, that I could be multiple versions of me at once: Professional. Mother. Party girl. That I could reside in the in-between.

I nursed beers while wearing old nursing bras. Handed out loose business cards from a baby wipes travel case. FaceTimed with my son from inside crowded classrooms, crowded bars and the back seat of my car after taking five-minute catnaps. I forced separate parts of my identity to coexist.

I wonder whether this is how the idea for "Sharktopus" originated.

The last night of the conference, I drove to my old college campus, a final push to prove I was still young, sexy, fun. To prove I still belonged. I should've known it would be a losing battle when the marquee for the bar we always danced at on '80s night read, "Tuesday: '90s Night!"

I wasn't alone in this venture. Three of my college friends joined me in the overzealous pursuit of momentarily incorporating our younger selves into the adults we'd become.

162

At the bar, a group of seniors celebrated finishing their final assignment before entering the adult world. They asked how old we were and laughed when we told them. "Aren't you a little too ancient to be here?" one of them asked.

Rounds of shots, spilled beer, sloppy dancing and a million songs on the jukebox later, we closed down our college town. Take that, 22-year-olds! The procreating professionals are in the hizzouse -- or whatever kids say these days.

The next morning, we had our answer to that senior's question. Holy hangover, yes, we were too ancient to be there.

While my friend puked up the previous night's ambitions, the rest of us explored new buildings that were built over the old ones we had attended. The campus was no longer ours.

I was in the university bookstore when my friend called to say paramedics were bringing her to the hospital for dehydration. She joked that we had done right by our younger selves. She, too, was an overachiever in the most ridiculous of ways.

Before heading to the hospital, I purchased a university decal to place on my car window next to my "baby on board" sign and my work's garage parking permit.

Sometimes being it all is not about proving it but about just owning it.

The Great Friend Migration

My friends have abandoned me.

I'm trying not to take it personally. But it's getting difficult.

With bands of my buds packing up their lives and heading back east in droves that rival Africa's great migration, I can't help but wonder whether I should have showered more often or not have let my pet rabbit gnaw on the cuffs of my pals' pants or have picked up the bill a few more times. Sure, my friends all claim to be moving away for jobs or family or opportunity, but it's really because I borrowed one too many DVDs that I never returned, isn't it? Isn't it?!

We had some good years, didn't we? The camping trips. The football games. The game nights. The nights we don't remember too well. The nights we remember all too well. Secrets stay secrets even if you're living in a different ZIP code, right?

To be fair, I should have known this day would come. I've always been absurdly lucky in the friend department, garnering and maintaining more friendships than any person should be allowed. And seeing as I know me, I feel qualified to state that I am no catch. The discrepancy between how many friends I have and how many I deserve is large enough to throw the entire Earth off its axis. Really, it's only fair to set the world right and leave me friendless on a Friday night.

Now, for the first time in my adult life, I am left with a chum conundrum. How do you make friends in your 30s?

I'd always assumed that by the time I was old enough to lose all my friends, my co-workers would have become my new besties. This proved to be a poor plan. I have great work pals, but to me, time with friends is supposed to be a break from work, not time spent talking about the office when you're not physically there.

I'd also imagined that in my later years, my children would be playing soccer on Saturdays and I could scope out the cheering parents for someone who shares my obsession for "Game of Thrones" and pineapple jalapeno pizza. Sadly, this plan, too, has backfired. My son turns 2 this weekend, and he can't even dribble a ball. His lack of viral-worthy gifted athleticism is really putting a damper on my social life.

Without my son or co-workers to rely on, I crafted five alternatives for finding friends.

1) Crash a bachelorette party. Positive: Instant access to a group of women around my age who totally know how to party. Negative: I don't know how to party. Not really. Not anymore. Unless the party wraps up at 7 p.m. with brushing our teeth to Elmo's toothbrush song. That's my jam!

2) Camp out in homes in escrow and yell "surprise!" when new owners move in. Positive: Seeing as the families presumably are new in town, they will be on the hunt for new friends, too. Negative: Potentially ends in a restraining order or my arrest.

3) Join a sports team. Positive: Exercise releases endorphins and will put everyone in a good mood to make a new friend. Negative: ...until my clumsiness makes our undefeated team lose a million games in a row and the team toilet-papers my house. Not that I know this will happen from personal experience or anything.

4) Join Tinder or OkCupid. Positive: I've heard I can state that I am only in the market for new buds. Negative: I've heard no one believes the people who state that they just want to be friends, and

my first play date may be at a hotel or in the back seat of my new friend's mom's Chevy.

5) Join a gym with classes. Positive: Make friends while getting a workout. Negative: You have to work out. No friend is worth that.

After carefully considering which of the five friend-finding techniques to pursue, I've decided that none of them will work. Clearly, no one has ever made a single friend without being at school, at camp or inebriated at a bar. It can't be done!

I guess that in the meantime, I can always just try being nice to people and see where that gets me. And barricade the highways so none of my other pals can leave.

~ ~ ~

Chapter 11

What a Messcellaneous: See What I Did There?

Traffic Tickets

I never have gotten out of a ticket.

Apparently, that makes me a bit of a loser. One of my dearest friends, Lena, is a savant at getting out of tickets. Her superpower is the gift of gab -- a bubbling, bumbling babbling of words that, once strung together, cops find altogether confusing and charismatic.

When we were in high school, Lena drove a white '88 Buick Skylark with cow seat covers that cops loved to pull over. But for as many times as Lena heard the sirens ring behind her, she rarely had to pay out. It didn't hurt that Lena was beautiful. And it absolutely helped that Lena had the spastic charm of a puppy trying to climb stairs. There was something inherently adorable in the way she'd struggle to explain why she was violating the speed limit. The coppers couldn't help smiling.

One time in high school, I was sitting shotgun when Lena was pulled over for speeding outside of Baltimore. At the time, we were rabid fans of a then unknown band called Good Charlotte (an embarrassing story in its own right). It was before the group had a hit single, before the lead singer married Nicole Richie, before they were covered in tattoos -- back when they had their original drummer and their angsty tunes played to the hearts of a couple of 16-year-old girls.

Back then, the guys knew who we were, occasionally inviting us backstage. We were hoping to hang out with the band that night and were all too aware that this amazing opportunity wouldn't happen if we showed up late for their set. Lena spared no time explaining our situation to the cop.

"I had to speed, officer. We are going to a bar in Baltimore to watch Good Charlotte play, and we're late. We can't miss it. We're like their groupies." And Lena flashed her Lena smile.

There are a lot of things the cop should've gleaned from this admission. One: Yes, we were aware we were speeding. Two: A couple of 16-year-old girls were headed to a bar. And three: These young girls described themselves as groupies, a term that we didn't understand at the time had sexual implications.

But instead of asking us about all of those issues, the cop just laughed at the Lena-isms that were thrown at him and let us go with a warning. We made it in time for the concert -- and in time to hang out backstage with the band.

Over the years, I have tried to hone my inner Lena whenever I've been pulled over. I would try to mimic her unintentional flirtatiousness, but I never have been good at flirting.

"Hey, officer. The roundedness of your hat really brings out the angles in your nose."

I'd try to mimic her exasperated explanation as to why she was speeding, but I always came off more entitled than endearing.

"I was speeding because I'm wearing high heels, which causes my foot to press down on the gas pedal. You must know what it's like to drive in heels. Right, sir?"

I'd try to mimic how she approached the cops with complete honesty, but it was never appreciated.

"Do you know why I pulled you over?"

"I guess, but it seems a little premature. I saw my speedometer, and I wasn't really speeding yet. If you held off for another minute or so, you could've really gotten me good."

I'd try to mimic her infectious smile and flailing arms, but I only came off deranged.

"Ma'am, keep your hands on the steering wheel, where I can see them."

No matter what I tried, the cops would just look at me, unamused. Then they'd hand me a ticket.

Yesterday, as a cop stood beside me writing up a ticket, I decided to accept the fact that I never am going to talk my way out of one successfully. I sat in silence, simply accepting my fate. And something amazing happened.

"OK, don't tell anyone," the officer said. "You seem like a nice girl. I'm gonna write you up for a lesser offense. Save you about $100. OK?"

I'm no Lena. But that, my friends, is progress!

The Savvy and Brave Interviewer

The email read:

Out of the hundreds of rÇsumÇs I received, I picked you because of your experience and writing talent. I'm eager to set up an interview at your earliest convenience.

The position was in the development department of a major cable network. I really wanted the job. And from the looks of the email, they really wanted me.

After a few minutes of idle chitchat, the interview began:

Interviewer: You should know that (major cable network) is a boys club. How do you feel about that?

Me: I can swim with the boys.

Interviewer: Are you married?

Me: Um. Yes?

Interviewer: You don't have kids, do you?

Me: Uh-h-h-h-. I have a son.

Interviewer: How old?

Me: Three months.

Interviewer: Yikes. Do you really think you can handle the responsibilities of the job?

Me: (Scowl.)

Interviewer: You know what? Forget I said that. In fact, disregard this entire line of questioning.

Two minutes later, the interview was over. He had all the information he needed to decide to keep looking.

And I say kudos!

Seriously, I'm impressed. In today's society, only an intrepid company would take such a bold stance against mothers in the workforce. All this equal opportunity mumbo jumbo has made us overlook the obvious: Moms make abysmal employees.

Let's review the facts, shall we?

It's widely accepted that a woman's breast size directly correlates to her IQ. The larger her bra cup the less likely she's Mensa. But with all of today's sexual harassment nonsense, companies no longer feel as if they can apply this truth to the hiring process. What I really admire about the cable network I interviewed for was how it not only embraced bra-cial profiling but also took it one step further. Some places simply look at a gal's rĊsumĊ to decide whether she's got the chops. Not this network! My savvy interviewer understood that because my rĊsumĊ boasted jobs performed prior to pregnancy, it was practically obsolete. My breasts had grown; thus, my interviewer accurately deduced that my brain cells had shrunk.

During my interview, I pretended to still be the same capable person, but I couldn't get past him! It's probably because I'm not so smart as I once was.

The negative side effects of hiring a progenitor are infinite and often unexpected. For example, the development job required a lot of writing. A lot of writing requires nimble fingers. With my slip-on pregnancy jeans, I haven't had to work a button or zipper in seven months. My fine dexterity has been compromised! Sure, I used to be a fast typist, but that was before my fine motor skills went on hiatus. I haven't checked yet, but I bet it's safe to assume I type 50 fewer words a minute.

In addition to lowered IQs and stiff fingers, moms suffer another blow to their hireability: big feet. Feet grow during pregnancy, which one can only conclude slows moms down. For life. And that's just not fair to our employers! A company has every right to want someone who can meet the position's fast-paced demands, but how can they expect a mom like me to hustle when she barely can shuffle her clown-sized feet down the hall? So much for hiring a go-getter. If there's one thing moms are known for, it's their inability to multitask and use time efficiently.

The real victims here are the companies that feel pressured to hire women post-pregnancy. Which is why I applaud this network's unconventional mindset. Who did I think I was trying to get a job in television development after becoming a parent? Everyone knows that motherhood is just another way of saying, "Hey, I'm old and out of touch." Sure, I got pregnant in my 20s, but my labor and delivery discharge papers came with an AARP card. The cable network at which I applied to work accurately recognized I am no longer capable of relating to the desired 18-49 demographic. You know, mine.

But what I truly admire most is the bravery of this network. It was brave enough to take a stand, fully aware that a new mom is often so emotional that she just might consider doing something crazy. A new mom just might be hormonal enough to sue such a cable network for discrimination.

Hmm, that may not be a bad idea.

Super-villain Red Pinky

I am the super-villain to the worldwide superhero known as Earth Day.

I never intended on inhabiting an evil lair made of chrome and nuclear waste, but clearly that is where I belong. For too long, I have brought genocide to the plant kingdom. Plants that have lived long and flourishing lives wilt in my presence. Just call me Red Pinky, arch-nemesis to anyone with a green thumb.

My super-villain origin story started innocently, as they often do. I was born to a nature-loving science teacher and raised to identify plants and birds and to have a love of all things coniferous and deciduous. But then, when I was 5 years old, the apple tree that had been planted in honor of my birth died. I felt so linked to the tree that I clearly remember thinking that I would die, too. And perhaps a small part of me did die that day -- my nature-nurturing part. From that moment forward, no plant in my possession has survived a season.

Like many super-villains, I spent years trying to be good -- fighting my fate as a maple murderer. I would buy plants with better odds of survival. Desert succulents filled my bedroom. My mom, knowing my track record, would buy me cacti. "Surely, even you can keep a cactus alive," she'd say.

And I'd want to keep my cactus. I'd desperately want to. I would show my affection by petting the cactus and hugging the cactus. My mom spent hours with me and a pair of tweezers pulling out prickers from my hands and cheeks. And though I was excellent at affection, I was not so hot with hydrating. And after a while, the cacti would die.

Earth Day always felt like an opportunity to change my fate. Perhaps this year, my thumb would fill with chlorophyll, and at long last, I'd be able to give back to the planet. But year after year, the holiday only served to reaffirm my status as the Jeffrey Dahmer of horticulture, the Charles Manson of agriculture and the Hannibal Lecter of Ch-Ch-Ch-Chia Pets.

On Earth Day, my elementary school would hand out tiny plants to take home and care for. The soil was always dark and moist. The tiny plant was always bright green and fragile. I would name the plant something like Frank, Harvey or Malcolm. I'd spend the hours daydreaming about where I would put my tiny little plant when I got home. But by the time I got off the bus, the only thing that would remain was the white plastic foam cup the plant, ironically, was distributed in. The dusting of brown dirt inside the cup was a cruel reminder of my failure to keep my plant safe.

The years rolled on, and my relationship with the photosynthesizing never improved. My mere presence would cause the woods to wilt. Suicidal sunflowers would bow the moment they were caught in my gaze. If I passed daylilies, they'd close midday just for a chance at survival.

I've been asked on occasion why I don't have a vegetable garden in my backyard. I respond: "Look at the state of my grass. Even grass dies in my care." This usually ends the conversation.

When my now husband and I first moved in together, I decided to give caring for a plant one last shot. We bought a small fern from Wal-Mart and lovingly, creatively named it Wal-Mart -- Walmy for short. I believed that the care we gave for this plant would demonstrate the care we would give to a child in the future -- an idea that I deemed absolutely absurd and ridiculous when Walmy died a few months later. So much for that idea.

he plant world has rejected me. It doesn't matter what I do. I'm always underwatering or overwatering. Not giving enough sunlight or frying. So I've adapted into my alter ego, Red Pinky.

But truthfully, I don't want to travel the world donning a red plastic mask, spraying plant life with Tabasco sauce and aphids. I want to be one of the good guys. I want flowerbeds and fruit trees and, for goodness' sake, grass. At least grass!

Maybe this Earth Day, I will try again, starting small to avoid mass damage. Perhaps a cactus. But this time, there will be less hugging and more watering.

Blood Green Thumbs

I guess it started when my son went all Mr. Miyagi on a bee.

I pointed out the stinger-happy insect buzzing around one of the many overgrown, unkempt rosebushes that now covered the majority of our pathway. My 20-month-old looked where I was pointing and snatched the flying bee between his thumb and index finger. He held it up to me as an offering of his love; I, in turn, screeched my head off.

My son let go of the bee, tears streaming down his face. I checked his fingers for the stinger, but by the look on his face, I knew he was only crying because of me. He was scared because I was scared. And I *was* scared. I looked at the lawn through yellow-and black-striped glasses. My yard was a death trap.

Perhaps it is time to admit I am one of "those people" -- the kind of people who rile up homeowners associations enough to pick up their pitchforks and attack, if only they could find our home behind the thicket we call a lawn. Dead in the summer, fall and winter, my yard is covered in rogue rosebushes and spiny grasses in the spring.

It didn't start out this way. There was a time when my husband would freak out if you left a ball on the lawn, because "it will kill the grass underneath." But then there was a drought. Then our sprinklers broke. One thing led to another, and here we are. The ugly-lawn house. On the plus side, I get reprimanded less for leaving sports equipment around.

I began enjoying being one of "those people." I liked imagining the stories neighbors concocted about us -- the kind I used to think of when I was a kid. If the weeds just grow a little higher, I thought, I may even get to possible-witch status. That would be cool.

But my lofty Wiccan aspirations were cut short. After the bee incident, I knew I had to do something about my overgrown vortex of death. Someone had to cut down the risk of the lawn reaper, so I grabbed my shovel and hedge clippers.

It started innocently enough. I snipped a few stray branches off the bushes. Then I cut the bushes back until they were covering only half the walkway. Snip. Snip. Then I cut the branches so they were not covering the walkway at all. By the time the path was clear, I was hooked.

Never one to garden before, I took to it like a teenager getting revenge on an ex. I was vengeful. Wrathful. And gleeful to be so. After the bushes were mere skeletons of their once wild, albeit beautiful, selves, I moved on to the rest of the lawn. Instead of bringing out the mower, I began cutting down the spiny weeds in my lawn one by one with the clippers, imagining them as an army out to attack my child. I actually began speaking to the plants as I cut them down to size.

"You think you can come here, to my lawn, and hurt my child? Is that what you think? Not in my backyard, buddy!" Snip!

I ripped up weeds, removed dead plants, broke off brittle branches from plants long dead. I saw everything as either waiting to impale my child or attracting something ominous so he would end up like Macaulay Culkin in "My Girl." My son will not lose his glasses looking for your mood ring, Vada Sultenfuss.

With each plant I pulled, I felt both more empowered and more embarrassed by how negligent I had been. There was a tree growing in my backyard covered in spines, each more than an inch long. What kind of parent allows that to grow in her lawn? Even the Lorax would grab a chain saw before getting all tree-hugger on that spiny sapling! It took me more than an hour of thrusting the shovel into the roots before I was able to dig up the killer tree and dispose of it.

When my husband came home, I ran over to tell him what a hedge-clipping rock star I was. To show him my actual green thumbs. (Who knew that was a real thing?) To gloat about how I had singlehandedly dug up a tree! A whole tree! But before I could, my husband said, "Hey, baby, happy Earth Day."

I hung my head in shame.

Feline Foes

I am a dog person.

Nothing makes me feel as if Earth is about to go spinning off its axis, flipping wildly into the abyss, more than folks who claim to be both a dog person and a cat person. Let me be clear: There is no such thing. It's like being an Eagles fan and a Cowboys fan. A Pollyanna and an Ebenezer Scrooge. A lover of guardian angels and of the devil. Not that I'm saying cats are akin to Lucifer, but to be fair, I think we can all agree they have a little gleam of evil behind their eyes. Though I can accept that perhaps a person can be OK with both species, cat and dog, cohabiting the planet, I fundamentally believe that every person has a preference. Anyone who doesn't is just unnatural -- clearly suffering from some mommy issues that should be worked out through intensive therapy.

Let me start by saying that I hate cats. I'm sorry; that was a little harsh. Let me try again. I hate cats.

Oops! There it was again. I'll try to rephrase:

I am a dog person. Purely, completely, 100 percent. Well, it used to be 100 percent. This past weekend opened my eyes to how the other half lives. No longer do I believe that all cat lovers are little more than foolish prey, unknowingly making themselves vulnerable to the catastrophic kitty uprising, in which all felines named Whiskers will unite in the dismemberment of their love-struck owners. Just some.

Catpocalypse may seem extreme to you, but my feline fears are rooted in personal experience. For a stint after graduating college, I lived with my friend Emily. She was a year out of college and had settled nicely into adulthood with a teaching job, a fiance, an apartment and three cats. I, on the other hand, was working two full-time jobs waiting tables, homeless and crashing on Emily's floor. A floor that I had to share with the enemy. Three of them.

I never liked Emily's cats. After all, they were cats. But my assuredness that felines are nothing but fur balls of malcontent was secured when I began waking up every night gasping for air, suffocating from the weight of the cats sitting on my face as they kneaded their claws into my shoulders. They'd hiss. They'd scratch. They'd unleash their homicidal tendencies by smothering the slumbering. It was a summer of scares. My fear of cats validated, my hatred of cats vindicated.

Ten years has passed since those days, but when my son and I went to visit Emily last weekend, I was greeted by the same three furry foes.

My son is an animal person. Watching him chase down anything that walks on four legs, I have had to come to accept that 1) he is too young to understand that though there is no wrong answer, he must decide whether to be a cat person or a dog person and that 2) being a cat person is the wrong answer.

For months, I have attempted to nonchalantly scoop my son off the sidewalk every time he has screeched in delight at the sight of a cat crossing our path, hoping he wouldn't sense my fear. But here we were, in the enemies' lair, and all my kid wanted to do was hang with the wolf in sheep's clothing.

My son is kind, but he isn't quiet. He is gentle, but he isn't well-balanced. He screamed in the cats' ears. Toppled over on their heads. Stepped on their tails. Chased them around the apartment. Drove the cats crazy. But my son couldn't tell.

Though my memory is filled with hisses and scratches and attempted murder through fur ball ingestion, the cats never once threatened or scared my baby. For the first moment in my life, I considered that cats may have one redeeming quality: selective homicidal tendencies.

Just as my defenses were down, I saw the viral video of the house cat coming to the rescue of a little boy who was being attacked by a neighborhood dog.

It was as if a cat took one of its terrifyingly long nails and sliced off a portion of my heart for felines. Now I'm 90 percent a dog person. That's probably as low as I'll go.

The ancient Egyptians regarded cats as gods, to be revered and feared. Shouldn't we trust the people who built the pyramids?

Let's Shut It Down

When I was a senior in high school, I took a creative writing class. My teacher was new, just out of college, and like many people starting out, he had big ideas with little understanding of the troubles they'd cause once implemented. Somehow, in the five years that had gone by since he was sitting at the desks where we students now sat, he had forgotten the rebellious urges. Forgotten the senioritis. Forgotten the Hulk-like strength of will that only teenagers and toddlers possess. He wanted to be cool. He wanted us to like him. He wanted us to marvel at what an amazing, life-altering teacher we had. He set his desired legacy into action by using the first week of school to introduce us to the movie "Dead Poets Society." Big mistake.

"Dead Poets Society" is a story about a bunch of teenagers stifled by the man until Mrs. Doubtfire inspires them to act out, buck the system and make their lives extraordinary. Teenagers who followed their hearts got the girl. The teenagers who listened to their parents -- namely, Red Forman -- died tragically. At least, that's what I took away from the film when I was 17.

For the next five months, my schoolmates and I skipped class as often as we could. All in the name of carpe diem, baby! (That Latin phrase sunk in more than anything I had learned in three years of French class. And this was during the zenith of Christina Aguilera and Pink's strutting around to "Lady Marmalade," singing, "Voulez-vous coucher avec moi?") We seized the day at every opportunity. We went out to lunch, to the mall, to amusement parks, to museums. Our teacher pleaded with us to return to class, saying he didn't want our many absences to affect our grades. But as far as we were concerned, by showing us the movie, our teacher had given us permission to misbehave. And in high school, the cardinal rule of no takesies-backsies was golden.

If the genie from "Aladdin" could quote Henry David Thoreau -- a poet who died 120 years before I was born -- in a movie that took place when my parents were little and hit theaters before I learned my multiplication tables and be able to send me and 30 other students into a rebellious tizzy, I ask you this:

What on earth is this government shutdown doing to our country's youth?

In all the endless babble and the constant rhetoric, I have yet to hear one expert, one journalist, one government official speak to the real victims of this crisis: the parents of teenagers. Can't you just see it? Hormonal, pimple-pocked, brace-faced teenagers manipulating this nationwide dilemma to their advantage. Doing what teenagers do best, making even something as huge as a government shutdown all about them.

"The government officials get paid while they're doing nothing, so why can't I get my allowance for doing nothing?" What are you going to say to that, allowance fairy? The kid has a point!

"Sorry, Mom. Can't walk the dog. Wish I could, but the government closed the parks." Poor Fido.

"I can't go to school. I'm sick with menin-malaria-gitis, and the CDC is closed. You don't want to be the parent who sends her kid to school with the ultra-contagious menin-malaria-gitis, do you?" No, you don't -- even if you are pretty sure it isn't real.

And we haven't even tapped into their rebellious actions. With firefighters possibly going on furlough, their teenage urge to pull the school fire alarm must be unbearable!

I get it, too. Why should the government officials get to play hooky when they can't? Come to think of it, why does the government get to play hooky when none of the rest of us Americans can?

I think it is only fair that once the government is back in session, it systematically provides every age group and vocation its own temporary shutdown. There will be a Teenager Shutdown Day. No teen will have to clean her room. Hot Dog Vendor Shutdown Day. Boil those dogs our own dang selves! Surgeon Shutdown Day. Replace your own dang kidney!

I'm going to write up my Every American Shutdown Day proposal and send it in to my representative. This is exciting! It's just a shame no one will be there to receive my letter.

Signs to Be a Stay-at-Home Mom

The first snowfall after earning my driver's license, I begged my mom for permission to drive to my friend's house. I promised I'd be careful, and my mom apprehensively handed over the keys.

As I made the right turn out of my neighborhood, I hit a patch of ice and began spinning. And spinning. I was unable to get the car under control, as was the driver of the truck that was skidding straight for me. I hunkered down, braced for impact -- shoulders pinched, jaw clenched, eyes squeezed tightly. But no smash came.

When I dared to open my eyes, I found myself in a parking lot, staring at a welcome sign on the doors of the Jehovah's Witnesses kingdom hall. The building had just opened that very morning.

It occurred to me that if I believed in signs, I would walk through those doors and convert. A bit of an odd choice for someone with a Jewish mother and Catholic father, but weirder things have happened. If I believed in signs, I'd have taken vows.

But I don't believe in signs. I didn't at 16, and I don't now -- even when the signs are about as subtle as a boy's purchasing a hotel room on prom night. If I believed in signs, I'd quit my job to become a stay-at-home mom -- a Jehovah's Witness stay-at-home mom.

The signs beckoning me to watch my son full time are like the nauseatingly bright ones advertising "Nudes! Nudes! Nudes!"; I may see them, but I choose to ignore them.

Two weeks before returning from maternity leave, the day care facility I selected mentioned they cared for unvaccinated children. Prophesying an outcome as dire as the Black Death or a "Here Comes Honey Boo Boo" marathon, our pediatrician urged us to place our son elsewhere.

The mad scramble for a new day care facility commenced. Leaving my son with a pack of wolves would be safer than some of the centers I saw. And I'm not talking about a pack of sexy wolves that turn into brooding shirtless guys. No, I mean the kind of wolves in "Little Red Riding Hood" and "Three Little Pigs" -- the kind that think humans taste like caviar. The day care scramble was scary and something I never wanted to relive.

Luckily, before returning to work, I found an amazing day care facility that I was happy leaving my son at until he was 37 years old and sending his own kids there.

There would be no such luck. The signs were too busy telling me to be a stay-at-home mom.

At 8 o'clock on a Thursday night, I got a call from my son's day care facility. The state discovered that the facility was caring for twice as many children younger than 2 as allowed. My son was out of day care. Effective immediately.

Frack.

The next few weeks were pure pandemonium. My husband and I checked day care centers before and after work while friends and family flew in to help watch my baby.

After finding a new place and paying my deposit, I brought my son by so he could get used to the new surroundings. That's when I noticed something bothersome. It looked as if there were more kids younger than 2 here also!

"How many kids do you have under 2?" I asked.

"Your son makes four," the caretaker said. "You're only allowed four."

"Point them out."

The caretaker pointed at six children.

"You just said my son makes four," I exclaimed. "You're over the legal limit!"

"Then let's hope the state doesn't visit," she said, and then she winked.

I was out of time and out of options.

A friend suggested day care in a Lutheran church. A bit of an odd choice for someone with a Jewish mother and Catholic father, but weirder things have happened. I checked out the school and fell in love. It was perfect.

I very comfortably left my son there and have been leaving him there for nearly a month. A home for day care, finally!

Last week, the teacher asked me whether she could mention the Easter Bunny to my son. She didn't want to make assumptions.

"Of course!" I told her. "I want to raise my son to know about all religions."

The teacher smiled kindly and said, "You're open-minded -- not like most Jews."

Frack.

Hey, universe, if you want me to be a stay-at-home mom, how about letting me win the lottery? How's that for a sign?

Zippy Grandmas

I am woman; hear me breathe hard and gasp for air.

It was brought to my attention that I have not really moved in 16 months. Excuse me, but I beg to differ.

I tone my quads daily by squatting down to the couch and then lifting myself off the couch. There's no doubt my abs get a serious workout by my lying down in bed, sitting up in bed and lying down again. And my calf muscles are fierce from working the pedals on my car. But yeah, OK, other than those intimidating workouts, I've been rather sedentary.

I hide behind my new job. My new baby. My new-age philosophy on accepting one's body rather than sculpting it. But really, I'm just hiding.

A couple of months ago, I began entertaining the idea of working out -- an exercise regimen for my brain, if you will. I then moved on to the proactive stage of setting my alarm clock for an hour earlier each morning. Boy howdy, did I ever get my biceps in shape hitting the snooze button every 10 minutes! I eventually graduated to getting out of bed, changing into my running clothes and then curling up under the covers for another 45 minutes before changing into my work clothes. To be fair, I think I've made excellent progress.

Then, this morning, I not only laced up my sneakers but also made it out of my house and to the 1-mile loop around a pond in a nearby park.

I'll hold for your applause.

Whenever I fool myself into going for a run, I only survive the idiotic journey by setting running goals for myself. Otherwise, I just run to the nearest ice cream truck and call it a day. A very successful day.

Usually, I will set my sights on something in the distance and tell myself, "I can stop when I reach that tree about two football fields away." But as I run, I opt to abandon that whole crazy tree idea and just run to the trash can one football field away. Then I realize that's insane and tell myself I can rest once I hit the park bench 100 feet away. Eventually, I just say forget it and start walking, clasping my fingers together at the back of my head as if I've just done something impressive.

That method works well for me. I have a system, and I like it. But that whole system goes up in smoke when I'm met by my running foe: speed-walking grandmas!

I hate those grandmas. I hate their little zippy strides. I hate their cute sun visors. I hate their floral pants. I hate that they walk in pairs. I hate their white shoes. I hate that they wear lipstick. And I hate, hate, hate that they smile at me as I run past them while gasping for breath. No one likes to be bested by a floral-clad grandma.

The problem is I let them and their orthopedics get under my skin. When I'm running in the bubble of assumed invisibility, I allow myself pathetically slow speed. I allow myself Humpback of Notre Dame posture. I allow myself multiple breaks. But if an Olympic-hopeful grandma is speed walking past the bench that I've intended to take a break at, I force myself to keep running. I straighten my back, quicken my speed, force a fake smile and choke out a friendly "hello" as I run past.

Once out of view from her bifocals, I double over from a full-fledged asthma attack. OK, OK, from a full-fledged out-of-shape attack. This always happens -- my face bright red, my legs shaking, my lungs imploding. And inevitably, those goliath grandmas catch up to where I'm doubled over and say, "Oh, honey, are you OK?"

Those jerks! I'm convinced that this is why the elderly are put into homes. We don't want the shame-inducing competition. It's them or us!

I've been bested by zippy grandmas before. It usually results in my going back to my couch squats.

Maybe I'm going about this wrong. I'm trying to beat the grandma gaggle, but maybe I shouldn't let my insecurities dictate my actions. Next week, I'll ask whether I can join them. I have been looking for a place to wear my floral pants. Added bonus: all the hard candy I want!

Dad Bod

Dear Dad Bod Movement,

You're onto something here. No, really.

To those unfamiliar with the term "dad bod," let me fill you in. A teenager -- yes, teenager -- brought the term into common vernacular when she wrote an article explaining how doughy is the new sexy. It speaks of the natural confidence a man projects when he could have a nice body but opts to eat two boxes of pizza instead. This "doughy is doughlightful" disposition, of course, is limited to men and specifically aimed at college-age men.

I'm not here to complain about how "mom bod" would never be considered sexy, even for those of us who actually are moms and forever altered our bodies in the process of bearing our babes. Nor will I lament a culture that makes pregnant women want to diet, per my column last week. This column will not be a platform to speak of body image issues or sexism in America.

No.

Instead, I say right on, Dad Bod. Truly. Under your horrible and highly disconcerting name is the right attitude. Having the confidence to let yourself go is attractive. Amen. Now we just need a similar movement for women!

Here are a few female body movement options, just to get the conversation rolling.

--Kool-Aid (Wo)man bod. The Kool-Aid bod exudes confidence. It's for women who don't stop at breaking glass ceilings; they knock down brick walls. It's for the woman who knows she is so sexy that upon entering any room, she yells out, "Oh, yeah!" And you know what? We can't help but agree with her. This classy broad cannot be limited to simply being defined by an apple or pear; rather, she rocks a pitcher shape. The Kool-Aid bod chick is always found with a smile on her face, decked out in her favorite shade of red. Sure, she has no neck, so her face and body seem to somehow meld into a singular sloshing middle area. But if you ask me, that just adds to her appeal. She's confident enough to consume so much sugar that she doesn't have a neck! Now that's sexy. Someone get me a glass, 'cause

I just spotted a tall glass of water (mixed with packets of granular deliciousness, of course).

--Bathleisure. Young men rocking the dad bod can often be found strutting their confident, absent abs around in the hot clothing trend known as athleisure. It's for people who wear sweats, workout shirts, sneakers and yoga pants even when they're not working out. And let's be honest; our studly dad bod guys canceled their gym memberships last year. Men who don't care enough to put on real clothes are so darn attractive. But why stop there? Ladies, I say we up the game with bathleisure. Why even deal with the nonsense of elastic waistlines when we can walk around in our ratty old bathrobes and slippers? Or if you're feeling really ambitious and sexy, ladies, you can always try the more experimental fashion trend called cathleisure. Nothing exudes apathetic confidence like being too lazy to get up and fastening yourself with a catheter.

But why stop at new body trends?

--Cap'n Crunch misstache. Big is beautiful -- especially when it comes to the amazing kempt mustache of the one and only Cap'n Crunch. The genius behind the attitude of dad bod is that these men are simply working with what they've got. A tad bit of grooming goes a long way when you're confident enough to rock what you've got going naturally. And there is no better example of someone's embracing his natural beauty than the cap'n's maintenance of his perfect 'stache. Which is why the Cap'n Crunch misstache will be taking the world by storm. No more waxing, dying, plucking or shaving, ladies! Grow in those upper-lip hairs. Grow them long, bushy and strong. Extra points if you fight the urge to dye your grays and let your upper lip be covered in a thick coat of white hair. Love your locks, wherever they might grow.

In conclusion: Guys, go ahead and enjoy your dad bods. You deserve it, you big beautiful animals. I'm sure that one day soon, women will also be basking in praise for promoting confidence. Give it a month. All you'll hear is: "Look at that hot bathleisure babe with the Cap'n Crunch misstache and Kool-Aid bod. Oh, yeah!"

Birthday Barf Bag

"Hey, love, how goes your birthday?"
"You remembered!"
It was 11 a.m. He was onto me. Shoot!

It's not like me to forget my husband's birthday. Birthdays are a very big deal in my world. I used to plan a week of events, starting with breakfast in bed. But here we were, in late morning, and I had only just remembered.

I considered the series of lies I could tell:

"They moved me at work to a place with no cell reception."

"How are you able to call me now?" he would ask.

"Oh, uh, I stepped outside," I would say, feeling that weird itch warning me I'm getting off too easily.

"Why couldn't you step out earlier?"

There it was, logic assaulting my lie. And then I would spiral.

"Baby, it's been crazy," I would say. "My boss needed all this work done, so they literally chained me to the desk. But I knew I had to call you, so I kicked at my wooden desk until it splintered. Used one of the wood fragments to pick the lock chaining me to the desk. Had to parkour past some armed guards and may have maimed a mime with a machine gun on my way out."

There would be silence on the other end.

"Was the mime too much?" I would ask. Mimes are always a dead giveaway I'm lying.

I should really consider fixating on another heavily made-up group of people. I think they come up so often because it is my subconscious telling me to *stop talking!* And to get caught in an invisible box.

I decided to be honest.

"I'm the worst. But I'll make it up to you tonight. We'll have a fantastic time."

I hadn't *really* forgotten his birthday. It was just a morning slip. Weeks ago, I had ordered his present, booked a baby sitter and made dinner reservations.

It was at an authentic Spanish restaurant we had never been to. Before ordering our first round of tapas, the waitress asked whether either of us had dietary restrictions. I mentioned that I am a pescetarian. The waitress enthusiastically told me not to worry. There were plenty of dishes for people who eat no meat other than seafood. She made a few recommendations, which we promptly ordered.

After our olives, cheeses, nuts and bread were consumed, our first real dishes were brought to the table.

A few bites in to my cuttlefish and lentil medley, I told my husband that I thought there was a possibility I was eating sausage. He dismissed my fears; the waitress wouldn't suggest a meal with sausage when she knew I only eat seafood.

He was probably right. The taste wasn't strong. I probably was just reacting to the texture, and there were a lot of strange textures in that dish. But after a few more bites, I insisted my husband try a bite.

His mouth dropped. "Uh-oh, baby."

I pushed the dish away from me, willing myself not to get sick.

We called over the waitress.

"I'm a pescetarian," I said. "And this has sausage in it."

"It doesn't have sausage," she replied. "It has ham."

I thought about that moment in "My Big Fat Greek Wedding" when the entire Greek side of the family gasps at learning that John Corbett's character's family members are vegetarians, only to have a Greek aunt break the ice by saying, "It's OK. I make lamb."

I really didn't want to get sick. Not on my husband's birthday. We never get a baby sitter. We never go out. This was special. But within 20 minutes of the end of the meal, I found myself pacing on the sidewalk, waiting for my husband to bring the car around and vomiting in a gutter as if I were back in college. Even if the cause is food poisoning, once you're in your 30s, there is no excuse for throwing up in the street. Across from me was a long line of 20-somethings waiting in line at some club, looking my direction with pity and embarrassment in their eyes.

My husband ran into the restaurant to get me a barf bag. They gave him a paper to-go bag, which disintegrated from my stomach acid as I filled it with sausage. I mean ham.

My husband spent the rest of the evening cleaning puke off his car's passenger seat.

On the plus side, I'm pretty sure that at this point, he's forgotten the part when I didn't remember his birthday.

Lost Voice

My voice has been gone for a week. People seem to like me more. That stings. I mean, not so badly as my throat does but, you know, still, ouch.

The Rasputin of colds, the virus and its mucus in my head just won't die, no matter how many times I try to shoot it in the face with medicine or drown it in orange juice. There have been many side effects to having my sinuses sidekick my senses daily. In addition to losing track of cough drops, tissues and issues -- not to mention being completely thrown by the discovery that we are now in the month of March -- I've also lost my voice.

At first, my voice mutated to that of a prepubescent male, cracking often, much to the delight of co-workers. My news reports, which had previously been met with eye rolls or with people's sudden interest in their phones, were now heard by a captive and giggling audience asking me to "say that word again." I would obey, only to have my voice crack on the same word over and over, never to succeed in getting my point across. As a humor writer, this created quite the mental conundrum. On one hand, a captive audience who laughs at everything I say is a dream scenario. On the other, the fact that I received this acclaim without saying a single joke was a bit of an ego punch. Perhaps it's time for a career change. I could play understudy to that kid from "Jerry Maguire." He must be hitting puberty right about now.

CORRECTION: My editor just informed me that he's now 24. I'm going to blame the head cold publicly. Meanwhile, you can find me crying in the closest bathroom, bemoaning my age and searching for wrinkle cream.

Over time, my voice evolved to a deep baritone, which, according to everyone I spoke with, was apparently very sexy. Why men like a woman who sounds like a man, I will never understand. The sensual (read: snot-induced) sounds of my voice were once again met with a captivated audience. People were even willing to stand close to me, throwing caution to the wind when it came to the superbug I was clearly harboring the way Professor Quirrell hid Voldemort on the back of his head. I can't imagine that my superbug would look much more attractive. Come to think of it, after weeks of being sick, I'm not sure I look much more attractive.

The most enjoyable thing about my baritone voice was how interested everyone was in what I had to say. And this time, unlike when my voice was cracking, people could actually understand me. They weren't giggling at the silliness. They weren't entertained without ever having to absorb the point I was struggling to make. My listeners could really understand me and seemed legitimately interested. I began thinking that perhaps my newly acquired audience was not the result of my voice at all. Maybe it was the content of what I had to say that captivated them. It felt good.

Then my voice evolved yet again. Only this time, it was motivated by a throat on fire. Clawing on the inside every time I uttered a word, my sore throat rendered me speechless. I was a Teller without the Penn, a mime without the cool invisible box, Milli Vanilli without the lip-syncing skills. Unlike before, when my every word was hung on, now I hardly spoke a word. One-word sentences, if possible. I feared I would lose the crowd I hard worked so hard for, lose the acclaim my flu-vexed voice had afforded me. Would my co-workers remember that I was a person with valuable things to say when my voice eventually returned?

Last night, I left a 2 1/2-hour meeting after not speaking a word. Heading toward my desk, two co-workers came up, putting their arms around me and saying, with complete sincerity, "You were a real asset in the meeting. Keep it up."

I searched their faces for sarcasm. There was none. I had not spoken, perhaps for the first time ever, and was given my first compliment.

Perhaps there's a lesson in all this. Perhaps not. The most wonderful thing about being a writer is that you don't need a voice to be heard. Thanks for reading.

--Katiedid Langrock

~ ~ ~

About the Author

Katiedid Langrock lives in Los Angeles with her main squeeze, two kids and a rabbit named Pig. For the past decade, Langrock has worked as a writer and story editor in the entertainment industry. You can see her most recent work on the television series "Project Mc2" and "Lalaloopsy."

She also created WriteInTheWild.com, where she uses her experiences as an adventure tour guide in the Australian Outback and years working as a story specialist to consult with writers and encourage them to access their optimum writing potential by taking a breather out in nature.

Langrock credits her family and friends for being by her side through every embarrassing moment -- and then encouraging her to write about it while insisting on their names being changed to protect the not-so-innocent.

~ ~ ~

"STOP FARTING IN THE PYRAMIDS" IS ALSO AVAILABLE AS AN E-BOOK FOR KINDLE, AMAZON FIRE, IPAD, NOOK AND ANDROID E-READERS. GO TO WWW.CREATORS.COM/BOOKS.

42972146R00113

Made in the USA
San Bernardino, CA
12 December 2016